Flooded Area and Plant Zonation in Isolated Wetlands in Well Fields in the Northern Tampa Bay Region, Florida, Following Reductions in Groundwater-Withdrawal Rates

By Kim H. Haag and William R. Pfeiffer

Prepared in cooperation with Tampa Bay Water

Scientific Investigations Report 2012–5039

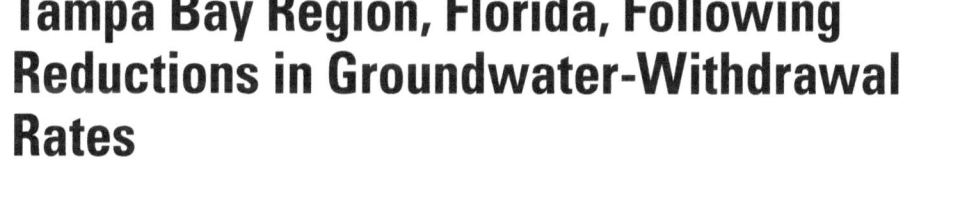

U.S. Department of the Interior
U.S. Geological Survey

U.S. Department of the Interior
KEN SALAZAR, Secretary

U.S. Geological Survey
Marcia K. McNutt, Director

U.S. Geological Survey, Reston, Virginia: 2012

For more information on the USGS—the Federal source for science about the Earth, its natural and living resources, natural hazards, and the environment, visit http://www.usgs.gov or call 1–888–ASK–USGS.

For an overview of USGS information products, including maps, imagery, and publications, visit http://www.usgs.gov/pubprod

To order this and other USGS information products, visit http://store.usgs.gov

Suggested citation:
Haag, K.H., and Pfeiffer, William, 2012, Flooded area and plant zonation in isolated wetlands in well fields in the Northern Tampa Bay Region, Florida, following reductions in groundwater-withdrawal rates: U.S. Geological Survey Scientific Investigations Report 2012–5039, 49 p.

Acknowledgments

The authors thank Brian Zumwalt and Douglas Keesecker of Tampa Bay Water, and Pamela Green, James Owens, David Carr, Michael Hancock, and Christina Uranowski of Southwest Florida Water Management District for providing historical hydrologic data and knowledgeable advice on area wetlands. Geoff Fouad, University of South Florida, provided assistance with wetland surveys and data analysis. Warren Hogg of Tampa Bay Water provided constructive technical review comments.

Numerous U.S. Geological Survey staff provided assistance to the authors during this study, including Suzana Hernandez, who assisted with wetland surveys; Amor Elder, who assisted in data analysis and prepared GIS products; Terrie Lee and Patricia Metz, who provided valuable guidance during the project and assistance in revising the report; and Scott Grotheer, Amy Swancar, and Arturo Torres, who provided insightful review comments that improved the manuscript.

Contents

Figures

Tables

Conversion Factors

Inch/Pound to SI

Multiply	By	To obtain
Length		
inch (in.)	2.54	centimeter (cm)
foot (ft)	0.3048	meter (m)
mile (mi)	1.609	kilometer (km)
Area		
acre	0.4047	hectare (ha)
acre	0.004047	square kilometer (km^2)
square mile (mi^2)	259.0	hectare (ha)
square mile (mi^2)	2.590	square kilometer (km^2)
Volume		
acre-foot (acre-ft)	1,233	cubic meter (m^3)
acre-foot (acre-ft)	0.001233	cubic hectometer (hm^3)
Flow rate		
acre-foot per year (acre-ft/yr)	1,233	cubic meter per year (m^3/yr)
million gallons per day (Mgal/d)	0.04381	cubic meter per second (m^3/s)

Vertical coordinate information is referenced to the North American Vertical Datum of 1988 (NAVD 88).

Horizontal coordinate information is referenced to the North American Datum of 1983 (NAD 83).

Elevation, as used in this report, refers to distance above the vertical datum.

Acronyms and Abbreviations Used in this Report

AD	adaptive
BM	bench mark
CBRWF	Cross Bar Ranch well field
CCWF	Cypress Creek well field
CIR	color-infrared composites
D	Deep zone
DOQQ	digital orthophoto quarter quadrangles
FAC	facultative species
FACU	facultative upland species
FACW	facultative wetland species
FDEP	Florida Department of Environmental Protection
GIS	Geographic information system
>	greater than
LiDAR	light detection and ranging
NOAA	National Oceanic and Atmospheric Administration
NP	Normal Pool
OBL	obligate wetland species
OD	Outer Deep zone
sp.	one undetermined species
spp.	multiple undetermined species
SWF	Starkey well field
SWFWMD	Southwest Florida Water Management District
T	Transition zone
TBM	temporary bench mark
TIN	triangulated irregular network
TPS	total positioning station
UPL	obligate upland species
USGS	U.S. Geological Survey
WAP	Wetland Assessment Procedure

Flooded Area and Plant Zonation in Isolated Wetlands in Well Fields in the Northern Tampa Bay Region, Florida, Following Reductions in Groundwater-Withdrawal Rates

By Kim H. Haag and William R. Pfeiffer

Abstract

The extent and duration of the flooded area were compared in two reference wetlands and nine wetlands in well fields in the northern Tampa Bay region, Florida, to determine whether reductions in well-field groundwater-withdrawal rates resulted in increases in wetland flooded area. Flooded area, expressed as a percentage of the total wetland area, was used to provide a quantitative and comparable line of evidence for describing the hydrologic conditions in isolated wetlands of different sizes and locations.

Flooded-area frequencies were quantified for periods with different groundwater-withdrawal rates that bracket reductions in well-field groundwater withdrawals. Four-year pre-reduction and post-reduction periods were applied to wetlands in Cypress Creek and Cross Bar Ranch well fields, whereas 3-year periods were applied to wetlands in Starkey well field. The reduced groundwater-withdrawal rates in Cypress Creek and Cross Bar Ranch well fields were 30 and 24 percent less than their pre-reduction rates, respectively. The reduced groundwater-withdrawal rate in the Starkey well field was 64 percent less. Total rainfall amounts were similar (differed by 1 percent or less) in the respective pre- and post-reduction periods, which minimized the effect that rainfall variability had on the analysis. Flooded-area patterns at the reference wetlands, which were unaffected by groundwater withdrawals, were similar during pre- and post-reduction periods, indicating that short-term rainfall variability within those periods did not affect the longer-term patterns of flooded-area extent and duration.

One well-field wetland (W-33) experienced an extent and duration of flooded area similar to that observed at the reference wetlands. About 61–100 percent of W-33 was flooded 41 percent of the time during the pre-reduction period and 45 percent of the time in the post-reduction period. The amount of time the wetland was dry decreased from 40 percent in the pre-reduction period to 26 percent in the post-reduction period. The median elevation of the potentiometric surface of the Upper Floridan aquifer increased beneath this wetland by about 4 feet after reductions in groundwater-withdrawal rates.

Four well-field wetlands (W-17, W-56, Starkey N, and Starkey 108) had substantial increases in the extent and duration of the flooded area after reductions in groundwater-withdrawal rates. These four wetlands were dry for 25–45 percent less time during the post-reduction period, when the pre- and post-reduction periods were compared. Up to 20 percent of W-56 was flooded more than three times as long after reductions in groundwater-withdrawal rates. All parts of W-17 were flooded for as much as 10 percent of the time in the post-reduction period. Parts of Starkey N and Starkey 108 were flooded for more than twice as much time after reductions in groundwater-withdrawal rates. The median elevation of the potentiometric surface of the Upper Floridan aquifer was about 4–8 feet higher beneath W-17 and W-56 after reductions in groundwater-withdrawal rates, whereas the median elevation increased beneath Starkey N and Starkey 108 by about 4 feet after reductions in groundwater-withdrawal rates.

Four other well-field wetlands (W-41, Q-1, Starkey D, and Starkey E) were mostly dry before reductions in groundwater-withdrawal rates and remained mostly dry after the reductions. W-41 was dry 23 percent less time in the post-reduction period, but most of the increase in flooded area was confined to less than 20 percent of the total wetland area. Q-1 was dry for only 12 percent less time in the post-reduction period. The median elevation of the potentiometric surface of the Upper Floridan aquifer increased beneath W-41 by about 5 feet and beneath Q-1 by about 2 feet after reductions in groundwater-withdrawal rates. The extent and duration of the flooded area was unchanged at Starkey D when the post-reduction period was compared to the pre-reduction period. At Starkey E the extent of the flooded area decreased slightly during the post-reduction period. Even though groundwater-withdrawal rates at Starkey well field decreased in the post-reduction period, the median elevation of the potentiometric surface of the Upper Floridan aquifer did not increase beneath Starkey D and Starkey E after reductions in groundwater-withdrawal rates from this well field. Factors such as the high permeability of sediments beneath the wetlands, subsidence, or sinkholes could contribute to continued downward leakage from these four wetlands and the lack of recovery of wetland water levels.

Plant zonation in the two reference wetlands and the nine well-field wetlands was described using data collected by the Southwest Florida Water Management District and Tampa Bay Water, a regional utility, in their Wetland Assessment Procedure (WAP). A scoring system was used to describe the distribution of trees, woody shrubs, and groundcover in zones at three depths along a transect line through each wetland. The locations of the three zones were identified on contoured wetland bathymetry maps and were discussed in relation to areas of the wetland bottom that flooded for different periods of time during the study. Higher scores are characteristic of a greater extent and duration of wetland flooded area.

WAP scores and weighted average scores for wetland vegetation were generally consistent with the results of the flooded area analysis. The WAP scores and weighted average scores were higher overall and did not decline with time at four wetlands in well fields (W-33, W-56, Starkey N, and Starkey 108) during the years following reductions in groundwater-withdrawal rates. These four wetlands also had increases in the extent and duration of the flooded area during the post-reduction period. Scores for trees were more consistent than scores for shrubs and groundcover. WAP scores remained relatively low or generally declined at five well-field wetlands (Q-1, W-17, W-41, Starkey D, and Starkey E) during the years following reductions in groundwater-withdrawal rates, and weighted average scores either declined over time or remained low. These five wetlands either did not have an increase in the extent and duration of the flooded area, or if there was an increase, it was small.

Introduction

Freshwater wetlands are a dominant feature of the landscape in west-central Florida and many wetlands in the area are small and isolated (Haag and Lee, 2010). Isolated wetlands in this area are supplied with water primarily from rainfall and runoff; rainfall patterns in the region have a substantial influence on the extent and duration of wetland inundation (Lee and others, 2009). Some of the isolated wetlands receive inflow from shallow groundwater, but most of the wetlands recharge the groundwater system, and the exchange between surface-water and groundwater systems is a dominant feature in the karst landscape of the region (Lee and others, 2009).

Hundreds of wetlands in west-central Florida are located in well fields (fig. 1) where groundwater withdrawals for municipal water supply are from the Upper Floridan aquifer. Groundwater withdrawals in the region have increased since the 1930s, and by the early 2000s, withdrawals for municipal water supply from the Upper Floridan aquifer reached a maximum rate of 165 million gallons per day (Mgal/d; Tampa Bay Water, 2004). The increased groundwater-withdrawal rates have lowered the potentiometric surface of the Upper Floridan aquifer and induced downward leakage from the water table in the overlying surficial aquifer (Hancock, 1999; Metz and

Sacks, 2002; Haag and others, 2005; Lee and others, 2009; Metz, 2011). Downward leakage from the surficial aquifer also has induced downward leakage from wetlands in well fields, which has altered wetland hydroperiod (the seasonal pattern of the water level in a wetland). This induced leakage typically reduces the extent and duration of the flooded area in many isolated wetlands that are located in well fields and in surrounding areas (Biological Research Associates, Inc., 1996; Rochow, 1998). Changes in flooded area extent and duration can alter wetland vegetation communities, and, in turn, alter critical habitats, rendering them less suitable for wildlife (Lee and others, 2009).

In response to observed changes in well-field wetlands, resource management efforts were made to develop alternative sources of municipal water supply and reduce reliance on groundwater in the northern Tampa Bay region, which includes parts of Hernando, Hillsborough, Pasco, Polk, Pinellas, and Sumter Counties. Use of alternative water resources, such as surface water and desalinated water, to reduce groundwater-withdrawal rates began in 2002 (Tampa Bay Water, 2008). Since then, the average annual groundwater-withdrawal rate declined from about 165 Mgal/d to about 96 Mgal/d during 2003–2009 (Christina Uranowski, Southwest Florida Water Management District, written commun., 2009). The subsequent recovery of water levels in the Upper Floridan aquifer is expected to reduce downward leakage from the surficial aquifer and allow expansion of the wetland surface area that routinely floods in well fields.

Regional water managers in Florida are required to allocate and regulate acceptable rates of groundwater withdrawals from well fields to minimize adverse impacts on wetlands in and around those well fields (Tampa Bay Water, 2000). Tampa Bay Water has developed an optimization plan using an integrated hydrologic simulation model. The hydrologic model, which is based on the physical characteristics of the surface-water and groundwater systems, simulates changes in water levels in response to groundwater withdrawals and rainfall (Tampa Bay Water, 2004). Temporal changes in groundwater levels occur in response to seasonal conditions in west-central Florida; as rainfall increases, infiltration of soil moisture and surface water (wetlands, lakes, ponds, streams) contributes to increased groundwater levels (Tihansky, 1999). Because increased rainfall can offset the cumulative effects of drawdown in the Upper Floridan aquifer and induced drawdown in the surficial aquifer, the effects of groundwater withdrawals on wetland water levels are less noticeable during periods of above-average rainfall and more noticeable during periods of low rainfall (Hancock, 1999).

Small changes in wetland water levels, which are routinely monitored at a point near the deepest part of a wetland and are referred to as stage measurements, can cause large changes in the extent of the flooded area because the topography is relatively flat. Water-level fluctuations over time at the monitoring point (plotted as the wetland hydrograph) may not be characteristic of the entire wetland, and cannot be used alone to estimate the extent or duration of the flooded

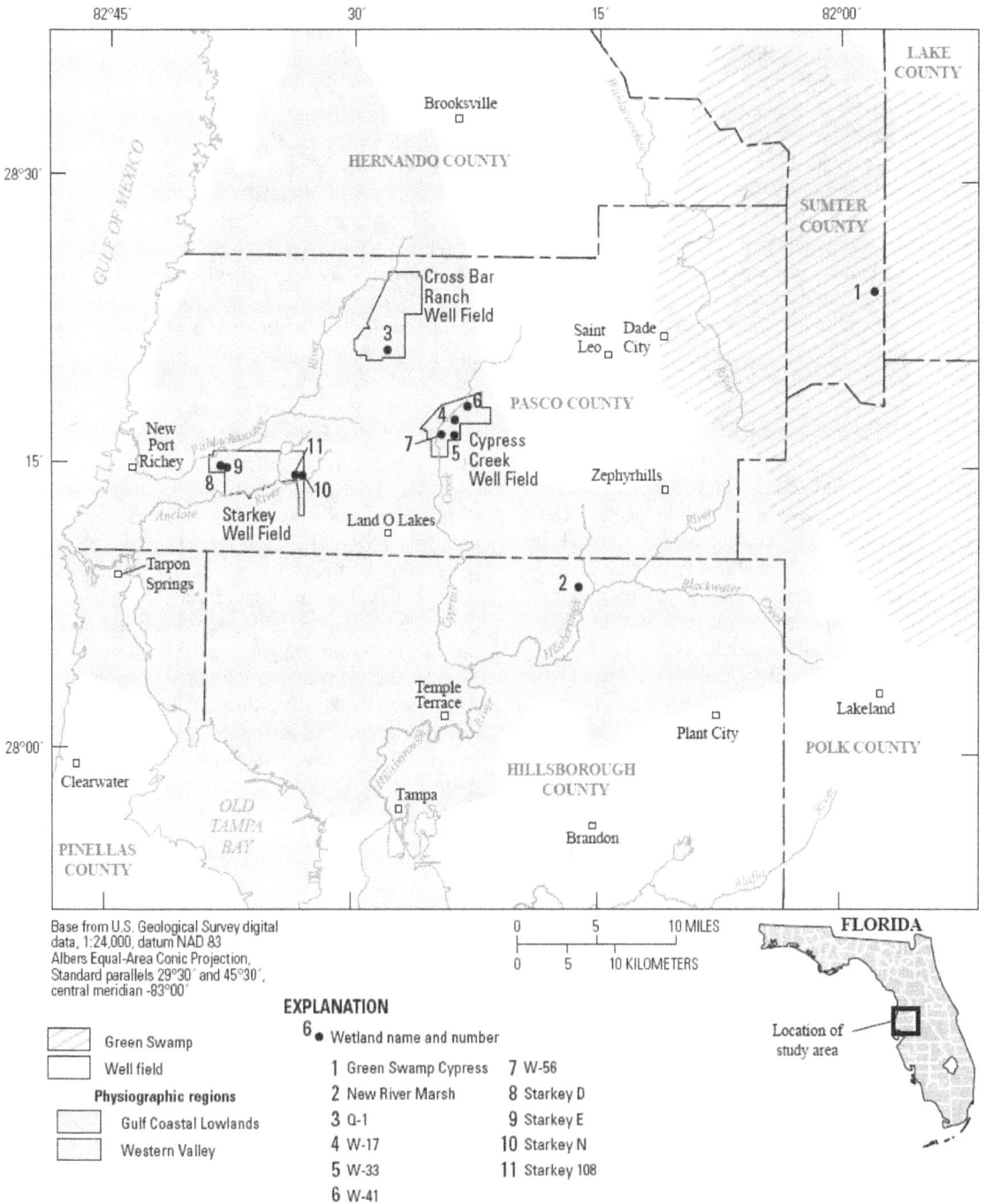

Figure 1. Location of study wetlands in the northern Tampa Bay region of west-central Florida.

area. Bathymetric data are a prerequisite for describing the relations among wetland water levels, water volume, and flooded area. Bathymetric data obtained by using standard surveying methods, or remote sensing techniques (light detection and ranging (LiDAR; Jones Edmunds & Associates, Inc., 2010; Lane and D'Amico, 2010) can provide the basis for estimating changes in flooded areas that control the distribution of wetland vegetation. Although hydrograph data for a particular year indicate water levels at the monitoring point, flooded-area estimates during a period of several years can indicate the amount of wetland area available to wetland plants. Therefore, flooded-area estimates combined with water-level data provide a more comprehensive understanding of wetland hydrology than water-level data alone. Flooded-area frequencies determined from wetland bathymetry and water-level data can be used to compare changes in the flooded area of wetlands for a given year, or different climatic cycles, or for longer historical periods (Lee and Haag, 2006).

Long-term changes in vegetation are the principal type of ecological evidence used to evaluate the condition of a wetland. In general, long-term monitoring is required to average out the confounding effects of cyclical rainfall patterns. Although changes in flooded-area frequencies affect the distribution of wetland plants and result in the distinctive plant zonation that occurs in wetlands (Rochow, 1998; Haag and others, 2005; Haag and Lee, 2006), a lag can occur in the response time of aquatic vegetation to hydrologic stressors, especially for long-lived species such as trees and shrubs (U.S. Environmental Protection Agency, 2002).

Wetland plant-distribution information is collected by Tampa Bay Water, Southwest Florida Water Management District (SWFWMD), and private consultants by using the annual Wetland Assessment Procedure (WAP) (Southwest Florida Water Management District and Tampa Bay Water, 2005). The WAP was designed to focus on the routine collection of data that can be used to assess biological changes in wetlands caused by the hydrologic effects of groundwater withdrawals in well fields (Tampa Bay Water, 2000; Hancock and others, 2005). WAP data can provide another line of evidence to describe the relation between groundwater levels, the extent and duration of the wetland flooded area, and the vegetation that creates wetland habitat.

In cooperation with Tampa Bay Water, the U.S. Geological Survey (USGS) initiated an investigation in 2008 to determine the extent and duration of the flooded area in isolated wetlands in well fields in the northern Tampa Bay region. Flooded area was assessed before and after reductions in groundwater-withdrawal rates, and the relation between wetland flooded area and plant zonation was described. Results of this investigation can increase the understanding of surface-water and groundwater interactions in wetlands. A broader understanding of the interaction between surface water, groundwater, and wetland ecosystems is an important component of the USGS Water Mission Area. An improved understanding of wetland response to groundwater withdrawals, particularly across the range of prevailing rainfall conditions, can assist in the protection and management of wetlands in central Florida (Torres and others, 2011).

Purpose and Scope

The purpose of this report is to (1) compare the extent and duration of the flooded area in isolated wetlands located in three regional well fields operated by Tampa Bay Water in the northern Tampa Bay region during a period before and a period after reductions in the rate of groundwater withdrawals; (2) evaluate the ability of the flooded area duration integrated over the two periods to provide evidence of the change in wetland hydrologic conditions; and (3) discuss the potential use of wetland flooded-area data to interpret long-term wetland vegetation monitoring data.

Nine of the study wetlands are located on three regional well fields about 25 miles (mi) north of Tampa, Florida, in Pasco County (fig. 1). Collectively, these three well fields (Cross Bar Ranch well field, Cypress Creek well field, and Starkey well field) cover an area of about 33 square miles (mi^2) and contain hundreds of depressional wetlands. Two other wetlands (Green Swamp Cypress and New River Marsh) that are not located on or near any regional well field were selected as reference wetlands because they are generally unaffected by groundwater withdrawals.

Wetland water levels were documented and summarized, and hydrographs were created from monitoring data provided by SWFWMD and Tampa Bay Water. Bathymetry data were collected to determine wetland size, depth, and shape. Stage-area-volume relations for the study wetlands were developed from previously recorded water-level monitoring data and from bathymetric data collected by the USGS. Flooded area of wetlands in the Cypress Creek and Cross Bar Ranch well fields was evaluated during 4-year periods before and after reductions in groundwater-withdrawal rates at these well fields (October 1998–September 2002, and October 2004–September 2008, respectively). Flooded area of wetlands in the Starkey well field was evaluated during 3-year periods before and after reductions in groundwater-withdrawal rates at this well field (October 1997–September 1999, and October 2007–September 2010, respectively). These periods, referred to herein as pre-reduction and post-reduction periods, coincide with periods of similar total rainfall reported by the National Oceanic and Atmospheric Administration (NOAA) for two National Weather Service rainfall stations at Saint Leo and Tarpon Springs, Florida (fig. 1), near the well fields. Flooded-area frequencies were interpreted with respect to historical records of rainfall, rates of groundwater withdrawals at the well fields, and potentiometric-surface elevations of the Upper Floridan aquifer.

Analysis of wetland plant zonation was based on WAP monitoring data collected by SWFWMD, Tampa Bay Water, and their consultants beginning in 2005. Using the WAP, wetland vegetation was monitored in three locations in each wetland along a gradient of water level from the perimeter to the deepest part of the wetland. Vegetation was evaluated by using a scoring system and scores were weighted using an ecological index value (app. 1). Vegetation monitoring data in this report for the reference wetlands and for wetlands in Cypress Creek and Cross Bar Ranch well field are for a 4-year period (2005–2008) after groundwater-withdrawal reductions began. At the Starkey well field, reductions in groundwater-withdrawal rates did not occur until 2007; vegetation monitoring data are reported for 2005–2010, but only the data for 2008–2010 represent the post-reduction period at this well field.

Description of Study Area and Selected Regional Well Fields

The study area in the northern Tampa Bay region of west-central Florida encompasses about 2,000 mi^2, and includes all of Pasco County and parts of Hernando, Hillsborough, Polk, Pinellas, and Sumter Counties (fig. 1). The study area lies in the Gulf Coastal Lowlands and the Western Valley (White, 1970). These physiographic regions have a relatively shallow water table and overlie the Upper Floridan aquifer, which is semiconfined or unconfined in this region. Nine study wetlands are located in well fields and the two reference wetlands are located nearby but not on well-field property (fig. 1; table 1). Land use and anthropogenic activities in the vicinity of the well fields have been described in detail by Haag and others (2005), and Lee and others (2009).

The Green Swamp Cypress reference site (site 1, fig. 1) is in the Green Swamp Wildlife Management Area, which encompasses about 75 mi^2 in Hernando, Lake, Pasco, Polk, and Sumter Counties (fig. 1). The area includes pine flatwoods and numerous cypress wetlands. Groundwater resources are undeveloped in this area and surface-water levels are largely unaffected by anthropogenic activities. Green Swamp Cypress is a long-term wetland monitoring site established by the SWFWMD (Rochow and Lopez, 1984).

The New River Marsh reference site (site 2, fig. 1) is south of the Hillsborough County-Pasco County line. No residential or commercial development is within at least a mile of the northern and western perimeters of the wetland, or within several miles to the south. The land is forested to the south and east of the wetland, and pasture and forested lands are to the north and west. Groundwater resources are undeveloped in the area surrounding the wetland.

The Cross Bar Ranch well field (CBRWF) encompasses about 12.5 mi^2 of land in north-central Pasco County (fig. 1). The CBRWF has been in production since 1980 and supplied about 22 Mgal/d of water on average from the Upper Floridan aquifer during 1997–2002. At the end of 2002, well-field production was reduced to an average of 14.5 Mgal/d. The CBRWF is a multiuse facility; some of the area within the well field is conservation area that is managed for wildlife, and about three-fourths of the acreage is a cultivated pine plantation. Several lakes and ponds are on the property as well as wet prairies, marshes, and cypress ponds. Some of these sites have been augmented with groundwater since the 1980s (Biological Research Associates, Inc., 2001). The Q-1 wetland study site is located in CBRWF (site 3, fig. 1).

The Cypress Creek well field (CCWF) encompasses about 7 mi^2 of land in central Pasco County (fig. 1). The land within this well field is relatively natural and is used as a wilderness park. The property has numerous isolated marsh and cypress wetlands. Cypress Creek, which historically flowed through the area now occupied by the well field, has been dry for long periods during recent years. Anthropogenic activities surrounding the well field include residential development and agriculture. The CCWF has operated since 1976 and supplied about 30 Mgal/d on average from the Upper Floridan aquifer before groundwater-withdrawal rates were reduced at

Table 1. Names, locations, and physical characteristics of study wetlands in west-central Florida.

[USGS, U.S. Geological Survey; N, north; W, west; latitude and longitude in degrees (°), minutes ('), and seconds (")]

Wetland number (fig. 1)	USGS wetland name	Wetland type	Wetland location	Analysis period	Latitude	Longitude	Size (acres)	Maximum depth (feet)
1	Green Swamp Cypress	Reference cypress	Green Swamp Wildlife Management Area	10/1/1998–9/30/2008	28°24'47"N	81°57'40"W	1.7	1.7
2	New River Marsh	Reference marsh	Hillsborough River flood plain	5/8/2001–5/8/2009	28°08'50"N	82°15'37"W	2.9	2.9
3	Q-1	Cypress	Cross Bar Ranch well field	10/1/1998–9/30/2008	28°20'44"N	82°28'11"W	1.4	1.6
4	W-17	Cypress	Cypress Creek well field	10/1/1998–9/30/2008	28°17'08"N	82°23'41"W	3.9	2.5
5	W-33	Cypress	Cypress Creek well field	10/1/1998–9/30/2008	28°16'34"N	82°23'34"W	1.2	1.5
6	W-41	Cypress	Cypress Creek well field	10/1/1998–9/30/2008	28°18'45"N	82°22'24"W	4.3	2.7
7	W-56	Cypress	Cypress Creek well field	10/1/1998–9/30/2008	28°16'21"N	82°24'18"W	0.7	1.6
8	Starkey D	Cypress	Starkey well field	10/1/1996–9/30/2010	28°15'20"N	82°38'09"W	5.3	4.7
9	Starkey E	Marsh	Starkey well field	10/1/1996–9/30/2010	28°14'39"N	82°37'60"W	3.4	11.9
10	Starkey N	Cypress	Starkey well field	10/1/1996–9/30/2010	28°14'32"N	82°33'09"W	3.9	1.6
11	Starkey 108	Cypress	Starkey well field	10/1/1996–9/30/2010	28°14'19"N	82°33'31"W	1.1	1.7

the end of 2002. Many wetlands in the well field have been affected by lower groundwater levels, and several have been augmented with groundwater for more than 20 years (Rochow, 1998; Berryman & Henigar, Inc., 2000; Reynolds, Smith, and Hills, Inc., 2001). At the end of 2002, groundwater-withdrawal rates were reduced to an average of 15 Mgal/d to lessen the impacts to wetlands in the well field. Four wetland study sites are located in the CCWF—W-17 (site 4), W-33 (site 5), W-41 (site 6), and W-56 (site 7, fig. 1).

The Starkey well field (SWF) encompasses about 12 mi^2 in southwest Pasco County (fig. 1) and consists of undeveloped land that includes pine flatwoods and sand hills, cypress domes, marshes, and wet prairies (Rochow, 1998). Land adjacent to the well field is mostly rural, although a residential development borders the western side of the well field, and a four-lane highway borders the eastern side. The SWF has been in production since 1975, and supplied 10–13 Mgal/d of water during 1997–2007 (fig. 2). Some wetlands in the SWF have been affected by well-field production whereas others have not, depending on the proximity of the wetlands

to the production wells and the local degree of confinement between the surficial and Upper Floridan aquifers, which is greater on the east side of the well field than on the west side (Rochow, 1998; Berryman & Henigar, Inc., 2001). Four wetland study sites are located in the SWF—Starkey D (site 8), Starkey E (site 9), Starkey N (site 10), and Starkey 108 (site 11, fig. 1).

Historic and Recent Groundwater Production

Groundwater currently provides drinking water for 90 percent of Florida's population, and the majority of groundwater withdrawals (about 60 percent) are from the Floridan aquifer system (Marella, 2009). In the northern Tampa Bay region, more than 700 permitted wells pump water from the Upper Floridan aquifer, the uppermost producing zone in the Floridan aquifer system. This groundwater is used not only for drinking water but also for agriculture, industry, and recreation (Metz and others, 2007).

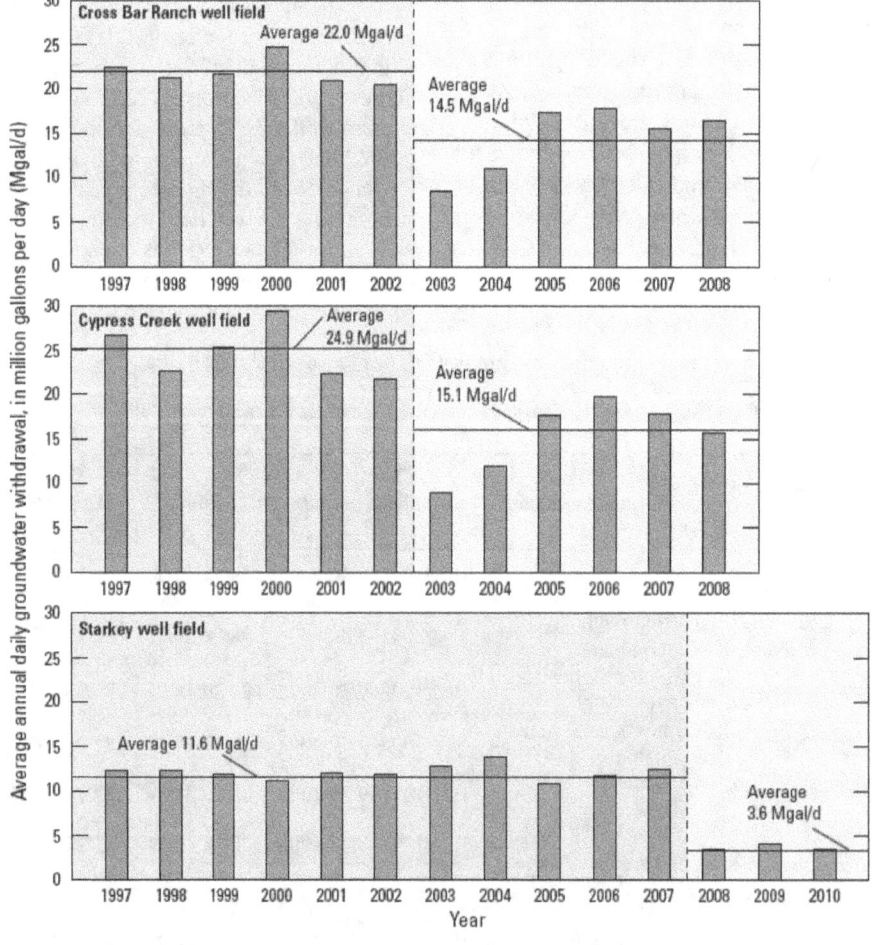

Figure 2. Average annual daily groundwater withdrawals at Cross Bar Ranch, Cypress Creek, and Starkey well fields in west-central Florida before and after reductions in groundwater pumping. Dashed lines indicate when reductions began. The abbreviation Mgal/d is million gallons per day.

Groundwater in the study area is pumped principally from a system of 11 interconnected well fields in Hillsborough, Pasco, and Pinellas Counties that are operated by Tampa Bay Water (2008) to serve the public water-supply needs for Tampa Bay area communities. The water supply for Tampa Bay Water prior to 2002 was exclusively groundwater. Tampa Bay Water made extensive efforts to reduce reliance on groundwater for public supply, and by 2006, 24 percent of the water supplied by Tampa Bay Water was from surface water. The completion of a desalination plant in 2003 by Tampa Bay Water provided a more diverse water supply. In 2008, Tampa Bay Water's potable water supply was composed of about 61 percent groundwater, 28 percent surface water, and 11 percent desalinated water (Tampa Bay Water, 2010). In addition to water-supply source diversifications, Tampa Bay Water plans and coordinates conservation measures to further reduce overall demand (Tampa Bay Water, 2011).

Since the reductions in groundwater-withdrawal rates were initiated in 2002, the average annual cumulative groundwater-withdrawal rate from the combined system of interconnected well fields declined from about 130 Mgal/d in 2002 to about 96 Mgal/d during 2003–2009 (Robert Peterson, Southwest Florida Water Management District, written commun., 2009). The magnitude of groundwater-withdrawal reductions at well fields where the study wetlands are located is shown in figure 2 (Robert Peterson, Southwest Florida Water Management District, written commun., 2009). Groundwater-withdrawal rates were reduced by 24 percent at the CBRWF and by 30 percent at the CCWF when the pre- and post-reduction study periods were compared. Reductions in groundwater-withdrawal rates at the SWF were not initiated until late 2007 when that well field was connected to the regional system. Rates at the SWF were reduced by 64 percent when the pre- and post-reduction study periods were compared.

The reductions in groundwater-withdrawal rates have allowed the potentiometric surface of the Upper Floridan aquifer to recover in the vicinity of the well fields. Box plots were used to compare the distance of the potentiometric surface of the Upper Floridan aquifer above or below the wetland bottom of study wetlands at the CCWF, CBRWF, and SWF during the pre-and post-reduction periods that bracket reductions in groundwater-withdrawal rates at the well fields and that were used to analyze wetland flooded area (fig. 3). Box plots were constructed to show the daily average elevation difference between the lowest point along the wetland bottom and the potentiometric surface of the Upper Floridan aquifer. Elevation data for the potentiometric surface of the Upper Floridan aquifer used in constructing the box plots was provided by SWFWMD from monitoring wells near the study wetlands (table 2) and are available at *http://www18.swfwmtd.state.fl.us/ResData/Search*. The elevation of the wetland bottom was determined from bathymetric surveys completed by the USGS during the study.

The median increase in the potentiometric surface of the Upper Floridan aquifer beneath the study wetlands at the CCWF ranged from about 3 to 8 feet (ft) when the pre- and post-reduction periods were compared. The median increase in the potentiometric surface at the CBRWF beneath site Q-1 was about 2 ft. The median increase in the potentiometric surface beneath the two study wetlands in the eastern part of the SWF (site 10, Starkey N and site 11, Starkey 108) was about 4 ft; however, the potentiometric surface of the Upper Floridan aquifer beneath the two wetlands located in the western part of the SWF (site 8, Starkey D and site 9, Starkey E) did not increase (fig. 3) when the pre-and post-reduction periods were compared; instead a small decrease (0.5–1.0 ft) was noted.

Rainfall Patterns

Rainfall data from NOAA for the National Weather Service Saint Leo, Florida station, near the CCWF and CBRWF (fig. 1), were summarized to help interpret wetland inundation patterns and the response to reductions in groundwater-withdrawal rates at the five wetlands in these well fields. The long-term average rainfall (1895–2009) at the Saint Leo station is 55.49 inches per year (in/yr; fig. 4) (National Oceanic and Atmospheric Administration, 2010). Annual rainfall ranged substantially above and below the long-term averages during the 12-year period from 1997–2010 (fig. 4). Annual rainfall was as much as 15 inches (in.) below average (2000) and as much as 15 in. above average (2003) during the period. Analysis of rainfall records from Saint Leo indicated that when rainfall was summed during the 4-year periods before (10/1/1998–9/30/2002) and after (10/1/2004–9/30/2008) reductions in groundwater-withdrawal rates at the CCWF and CBRWF, total rainfall amounts (187.0 and 184.4 in., respectively) differed by about 1 percent (table 3A). These 4-year periods were used to describe changes in wetland flooded area because of the parity in total rainfall.

Rainfall data from NOAA for the National Weather Service Tarpon Springs, Florida station, near the SWF (fig. 1), was summarized to help interpret wetland inundation patterns and the response to reductions in groundwater-withdrawal rates at the four wetlands in this well field. The long-term average rainfall (1892–2009) at the Tarpon Springs station is 51.74 in/yr (fig. 4) (National Oceanic and Atmospheric Administration, 2010). Annual rainfall ranged substantially above and below the long-term averages during the 12-year period from 1997–2010 (fig. 4). For example, annual rainfall was as much as 15 in. below average (2007) and as much as 15 in. above average (1997) during the period. Analysis of rainfall records from Tarpon Springs indicated that when rainfall was summed during two 3-year periods before (10/1/1996–9/30/1999) and after (10/1/2007–9/30/2010) reductions in groundwater-withdrawal rates at the SWF, total rainfall amounts (169.8 in and 169.4 in., respectively) differed by less than 1 percent (table 3B). These 3-year periods were used to describe changes in wetland flooded area because of the parity in total rainfall.

Table 2. Characteristics of wells used to determine the elevation difference between the wetland bottom and the potentiometric surface of the Upper Floridan aquifer before and after reductions in groundwater-withdrawal rates.

[UFA, Upper Floridan aquifer; –, unknown casing depth; CBR, Cross Bar Ranch well field; CCWF, Cypress Creek well field]

Well field	Well identification number	Well name	Total well depth (feet)	Total well cased interval (feet)	Wetland name
Cross Bar Ranch	282035082283701	CBR-SRW-d	703	146	Q-1
Cypress Creek	281622082241301	Cypress Creek Deep 3	352	136	W-33, W-56
Cypress Creek	281845082224001	CCWF-TMR-2 Deep	625	–	W-41
Cypress Creek	281746082233701	CCWF-TMR-3 Deep	625	160	W-17
Starkey	281500082350402	Starkey 10 Deep	392	153	Starkey D, Starkey E
Starkey	281458082330701	Starkey PZ-5	703	146	Starkey N, Starkey 108

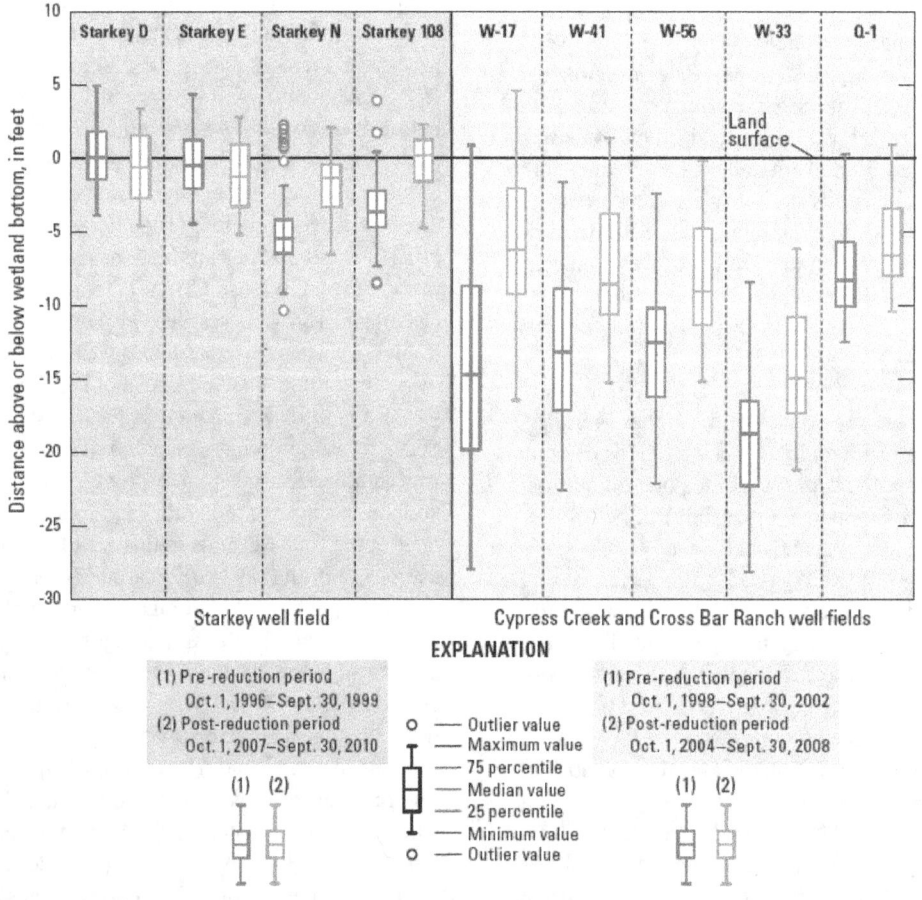

Figure 3. Box plots comparing the daily average distance of the potentiometric surface of the Upper Floridan aquifer above or below the bottom of study wetlands on well fields in west-central Florida before (pre-reduction period) and after (post-reduction period) reductions in groundwater withdrawals.

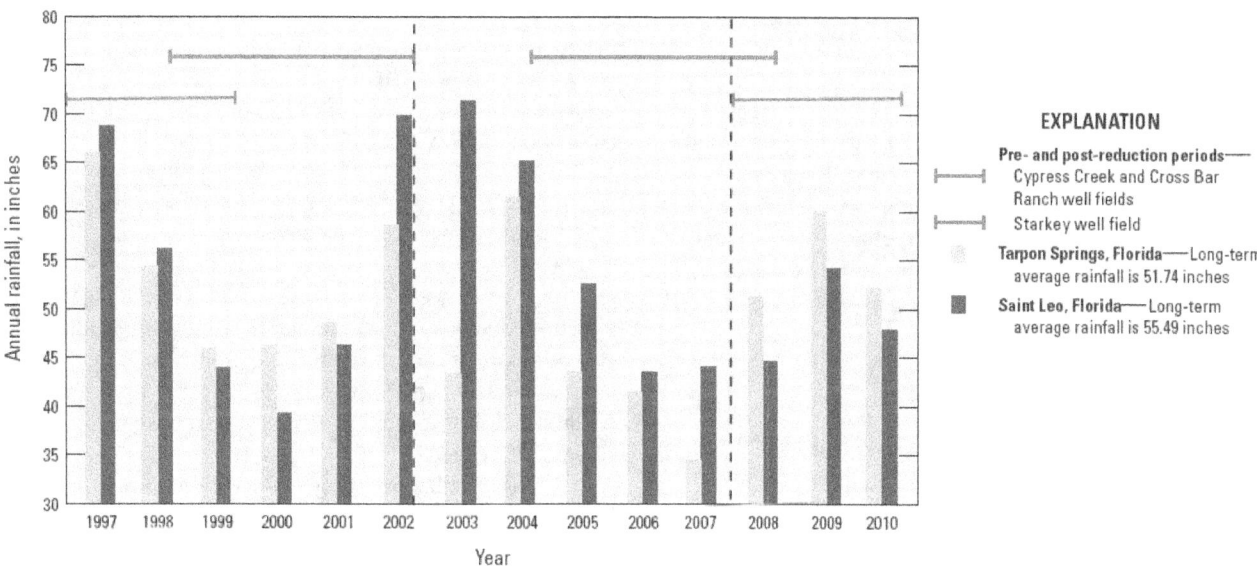

Figure 4. Annual rainfall at Tarpon Springs, Florida and Saint Leo, Florida, 1997–2010. Dashed lines indicate when reductions in groundwater pumping were initiated at Cypress Creek and Cross Bar Ranch well fields (September 2002) and at Starkey well field (December 2007).

Table 3A. Total rainfall at Saint Leo, Florida, during the pre-reduction and post-reduction periods when flooded area was determined at Cypress Creek and Cross Bar Ranch well fields.

Pre-reduction period		Post-reduction period	
Water Year[1]	Rainfall, in inches	Water Year	Rainfall, in inches
1999	41.33	2005	47.83
2000	45.47	2006	44.71
2001	45.90	2007	41.72
2002	54.30	2008	50.16
Total	187.00		184.42

[1]October 1 – September 30

Table 3B. Total rainfall at Tarpon Springs, Florida, during the pre-reduction and post-reduction periods when flooded area was determined at Starkey well field.

Pre-reduction period		Post-reduction period	
Water Year[1]	Rainfall, in inches	Water Year	Rainfall, in inches
1997	47.33	2008	53.64
1998	77.34	2009	55.60
1999	45.16	2010	60.14
Total	169.83		169.38

[1]October 1 – September 30

Methods of Data Collection and Analysis

The wetlands in this study (table 1) had an established staff gage with a period of record of at least 10 years to quantify surface-water levels, and monitor wells in or adjacent to the wetland with a period of record of at least 10 years to measure water levels in the surficial aquifer. The one exception is New River Marsh, which had an 8-year period of record.

Wetland Flooded Area

Surface-water and groundwater-level data used in the study were collected by the SWFWMD, Tampa Bay Water, and private consultants. Historical and recent monthly or bimonthly groundwater and surface-water levels were analyzed to describe the hydrology of the study wetlands. Water levels for each wetland were measured at the staff gage, and water levels in the surficial aquifer were measured in a wetland monitor well. Stage data and water-level data from the wetland well were used together to construct hydrographs for the study wetlands. When water levels were below land surface, the hydrograph shows data from the wetland well.

Bathymetry data were collected to determine wetland size, depth, and shape; to determine the stage-area and stage-volume relations of each wetland; and to determine wetland flooded area. Bathymetric data were collected by the USGS in 2009 at each wetland using standard survey techniques (Kennedy, 2010). The saw palmetto (*Serenoa repens*) fringe was used as a vegetative indicator of the wetland perimeter, and the elevations of the moss collar and (or) cypress buttress swelling also were used as vegetative indicators of the wetland perimeter at sites where the palmetto fringe was not continuous

(Carr and others, 2006). Aerial images in color-infrared (CIR) composites (digital orthophoto quarter quadrangles, DOQQ) were used to confirm field observations of the location of the wetland perimeter at some sites where vegetative indicators were not as readily apparent or easily accessible.

Wetland bathymetric surveys were done as follows. A position nearby or within the wetland perimeter was selected to serve as a viewpoint for an electronic total positioning station (TPS) (Topcon GTS 303D™) at each site. The viewpoint locations were chosen to maximize a clear line of sight in all directions and obtain the optimum horizontal range allowed. A maximum number of observations from a single viewpoint minimizes survey traversing, a potential for error. The wetland size and vegetation density determined the number of viewpoints needed.

A large number of survey markers with third order accuracy for elevation have been established at the CCWF, providing a local vertical reference at three of the wetland sites in this study (Jim Owens, Southwest Florida Water Management District, written commun., 2009). A steel spike was driven into the ground in an open (unvegetated) area to serve as a temporary bench mark (TBM) at sites with no nearby established bench mark (BM). The elevation of the TBM or BM was measured with the total station, along with any other reference locations, such as monitoring wells or staff gages. These established locations aided in georeferencing the wetland as well as determining elevation offsets to historic elevation data. During surveying, a differentially corrected global positioning system (GPS) was set up over the TBM to collect satellite observations for a minimum of 4 hours (Trimble 5700 Global Positioning System receiver with a Zephyr geodetic antenna) to provide a vertical (North American Vertical Datum of 1988, NAVD 88) and horizontal (North American Datum of 1983, NAD 83) datum reference point. The horizontal locations of points along the wetland perimeter were measured

Staff gage and wetland monitor well at W-41.

Palmetto fringe at wetland perimeter of W-33.

at approximately equidistant intervals (about 10 ft) generally starting in a northerly direction and moving clockwise. Elevations were typically measured along 30-degree radial transects extending from the viewpoint, at about 10-ft intervals (Wilcox and Huertos, 2005). At the largest and most densely vegetated wetlands, a greater number of viewpoints were needed, and temporary reference markers were established to improve accuracy.

The GPS reference point and TPS survey data were interfaced with a geographic information system (GIS). The arbitrary coordinates from the TPS survey were georeferenced with the GPS data and subsequently layered over CIR DOQQ aerial images. The bathymetry points were projected in ArcGIS™ using a combination of orthorectification and ground control point techniques (monitor wells, staff gages, bench marks) (Brian Zumwalt, Tampa Bay Water, written commun., 2009; Pamela Green, Southwest Florida Water Management District, written commun., 2009), The bathymetry points were then converted into a triangulated irregular network (TIN) and subsequently interpolated into three-dimensional continuous raster surfaces using the Top to Raster tool in ArcGIS™ (Hutchinson and Gessler, 1994). Continuous surface data interpolation allowed for the computation of spatial variables, including wetland volume and flooded area at specified stage elevations (apps. 2–12).

Flooded-area frequencies were calculated as follows. Bathymetric maps of the 11 wetlands were used to determine the maximum size of the flooded area (or inundated area) for the study wetlands over a range of stage values. Digital interpolation and contouring routines were used to delineate the outline of the flooded area at different values of wetland stage, and these flooded areas are herein referred to as wetland increments. The wetland increments are labeled dry (or 0), greater than 0–20, 21–40, 41–60, 61–80, and 81–100 percent of the total wetland area. The hydrograph data were used to determine the amount of time that wetland water levels reached a specified elevation, and therefore the duration of inundation (or flooding) in each of these increments of wetland area. The duration of inundation is referred to in percent of time (0–100 percent of the 3-year or 4-year study period), and if the percent of time is less than 25 percent, the number of weeks is included to provide a context for the reader.

Flooded-area frequencies for the pre-reduction and post-reduction periods were compared for each wetland. Pre- and post-reduction periods with similar rainfall were selected for analysis to minimize the effect of rainfall variability on the results, and highlight differences due to groundwater-withdrawal rates. Three- and 4-year periods were used to minimize the effects of shorter term wet and dry cycles on wetland flooded area. However, rainfall has a strong effect on wetland water levels, and given the available record, it was not possible to select pre- and post-reduction periods with exactly the same rainfall patterns and antecedent conditions. Using 3- or 4-year periods with similar rainfall eliminates some of the variability in wetland flooded area due to rainfall, but not all.

Plant Zonation

Plant zonation was evaluated in this study using WAP data. The original WAP was described in the Environmental Management Plan developed by Tampa Bay Water (2000). WAP data were collected twice yearly (spring and fall) during 2000–2004. A detailed analysis by the SWFWMD of a WAP data subset collected during that period indicated variability in the results, and the WAP procedure was revised (Hancock and others, 2005). The revised WAP has been in use since 2005. WAP data collected during 2005–2010 were used in the present study to evaluate the effects of wetland flooded area after reductions in groundwater-withdrawal rates. Data collected prior to 2005 are not comparable to the WAP data collected during 2005–2010 due to modifications in the scoring scale and scoring criteria (Hancock and others, 2005).

The WAP data are collected along a transect from the wetland edge to the deepest part of the wetland (fig. 5). The cover, composition, and zonation of the most common ground-cover, shrub, and tree species are assessed and ranked from a low of 1 to a high of 5 (Hancock and others, 2005), with the highest scores indicating expected zonation in unimpacted wetlands. The wetland edge and the normal pool elevation used in the WAP are established for each wetland according to WAP protocols (Hancock and others, 2005). The SWFWMD developed the concept of a normal pool elevation for isolated wetlands in the northern Tampa Bay region to establish a standard elevation datum that would facilitate comparisons of hydrology among wetlands (Hull and others, 1989). The normal pool elevation can be identified consistently in the northern Tampa Bay region using vegetative indicators of sustained inundation (Schultz and others, 2004; Carr and others, 2006). The normal pool elevation also has been described by Tampa Bay Water as the average water-level elevation in a non-impacted wetland during a year of average rainfall (Tampa Bay Water, 2000).

Survey tripod for collection of bathymetry data in the densely vegetated interior of W-56.

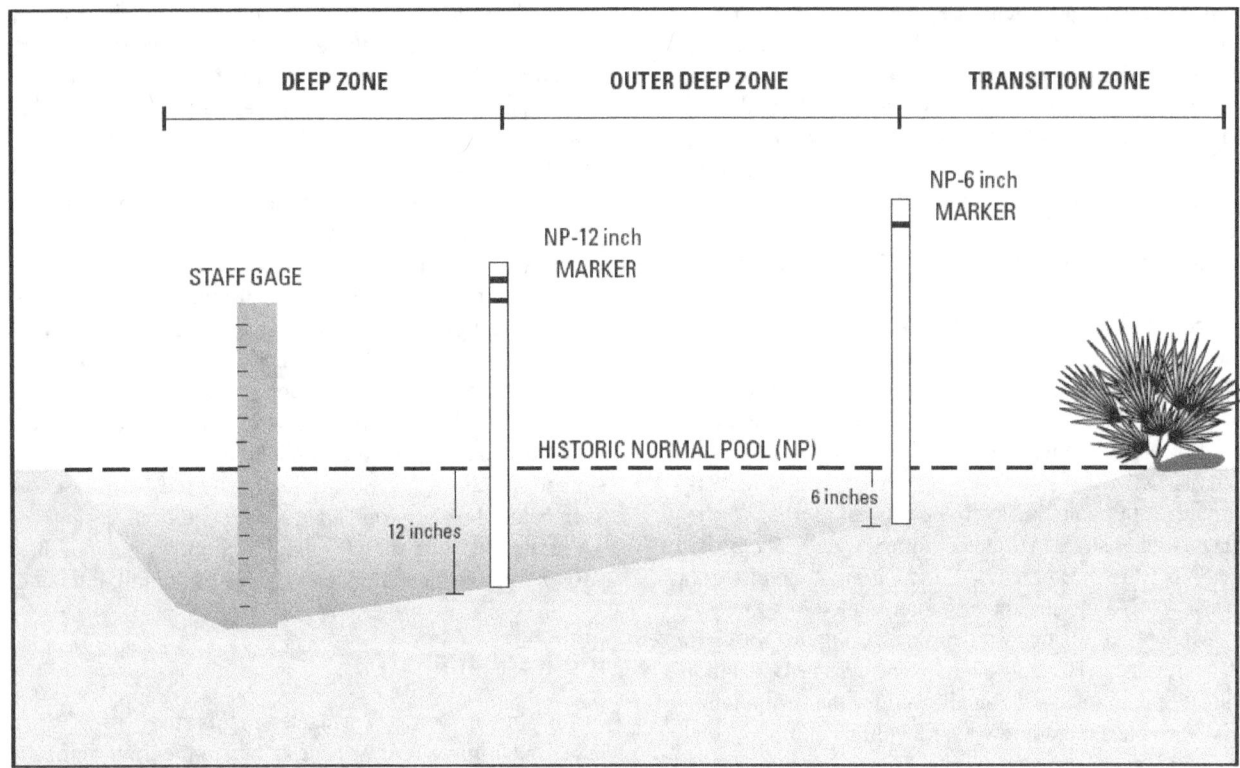

Figure 5. Wetland Assessment Procedure (WAP) transect with vegetation zones (modified from Willis and Schmutz, 2008).

The mean percent cover of the five dominant plant species in each of three WAP zones in each wetland was compiled. The WAP zones are Transition, Outer Deep, and Deep (fig. 5). The Transition zone extends from the wetland perimeter to an elevation of 6 in. below the normal pool elevation. The Outer Deep zone extends from 6 in. to 12 in. below the normal pool elevation. The Deep zone extends from the Outer Deep zone to the deepest part of the wetland. A weighted average was determined for each wetland zone (Atkinson and others, 1993; Balcombe and others, 2005; Toth, 2005; Dwire and others, 2006). The weighted average was calculated by weighting the percent cover of the dominant plant species with an ecological index value for each species (Wentworth and others, 1988).

The ecological index values used in this report are based on the Wetland Indicator Categories defined by Reed (1988). An obligate wetland (OBL) species is present almost always (estimated probability greater than 99 percent) under natural conditions in wetlands. A facultative wetland (FACW) species usually is present in wetlands (estimated probability 67–99 percent), but can be present in non-wetlands. A facultative (FAC) species is equally likely to be present in wetlands or non-wetlands (estimated probability 34–66 percent). A facultative upland (FACU) species usually is present in non-wetlands (estimated probability 67–99 percent), but can be present in wetlands (estimated probability 1–33 percent).

An obligate upland (UPL) species is present almost always (estimated probability greater than 99 percent) under natural conditions in non-wetlands in the region specified. Although both OBL and FACW species are widely recognized as useful indicators of wetlands, FAC species are not considered to be reliable indicators of wetlands. Plant species discussed in this report (app. 1) are identified by common name and scientific name at the first occurrence; only the common name is used thereafter. Plants were assigned to Wetland Indicator Categories according to those used by Florida Department of Environmental Protection (FDEP) as reported in the Florida Atlas of Vascular Plants (Wunderlin and Hansen, 2010), and were given a numeric ecological indicator value as follows: OBL=5, FACW=4, FAC=3, UPL=1. If a FACW species was listed as transitional (T) in the Field Identification Guide to Plants Used in the Wetland Assessment Procedure (Biological Research Associates, Inc., and Berryman & Henigar, Inc., 2006), then its ecological indicator value was decreased to 3, because data indicate that in the northern Tampa Bay region those species were in the Transition zone but no deeper. Likewise, if a FAC species was listed as T or adaptive (AD), its ecological indicator value was decreased to 2, because data indicate that those species are present in limited numbers in the Transition zone. Higher weighted averages in this report indicate vegetation that is more common in wetlands than in uplands.

Changes in Wetland Flooded Area Following Reductions in Groundwater-Withdrawal Rates

Flooded-area frequencies were compared during pre-reduction and post-reduction periods for reference wetlands and well-field wetlands. Reductions in groundwater-withdrawal rates were initiated at the CCWF and CBRWF in September 2002, whereas reductions in groundwater-withdrawal rates were initiated at the SWF in December 2007. Total annual rainfall differed by 1 percent or less at the rainfall stations nearest to the wetlands during the pre-reduction and post-reduction periods.

Green Swamp Cypress

The reference wetland Green Swamp Cypress is distant from groundwater withdrawals in well fields and largely unaffected by development. Green Swamp Cypress is a small (1.7 acre) shallow (1.7 ft) wetland (fig. 6A) in the Green Swamp Wildlife Management Area (site 1, fig. 1). Hydrologic conditions have been monitored in the wetland since 1979 (Rochow and Lopez, 1984), and monitoring results indicate that the hydrology is typical for isolated cypress wetlands unaffected by groundwater withdrawals (Michael Hancock, Southwest Florida Water Management District, unpub. data, 2009). Lee and others (2009) documented the inundation patterns at Green Swamp Cypress during 1988–2003, and reported that the wetland was dry for about 50 percent of the time and more than half of the total wetland area was flooded for about 40 percent of the time. Lee and others (2009) also reported that two other natural cypress wetlands were flooded at the deepest point 7.9–10.8 months of the year and more than half of the total wetland area at those cypress wetlands was flooded 41–51 percent of the year. Studies by Berryman & Henigar, Inc. (1995, 2000) reported that several cypress wetlands unaffected by groundwater withdrawals were dry for about 29 percent of the period of record.

The extent and duration of the flooded area for Green Swamp Cypress during the present study were similar to patterns of flooded area reported by Lee and others (2009) for the wetland, and wetland water levels often reached normal pool (fig. 6B). The extent and duration of the flooded area at Green Swamp Cypress were consistent during the two 4-year periods applied to wetlands in the CCWF and CBRWF, indicating that variability in rainfall during the pre-and post-reduction periods did not affect flooded area frequencies of this unimpacted wetland. The wetland was dry 44 percent of the time during the pre-reduction period. Up to 20 percent of the wetland was flooded for 15 percent of the time (about 31 weeks) and 81–100 percent of the wetland was flooded for about 26 percent of the time. During the post-reduction period, the wetland was dry 40 percent of the time. Up to 20 percent of the wetland was flooded for 17 percent of the time (about 35 weeks), and 81–100 percent of the wetland was flooded 25 percent of the time (fig. 6C, D).

New River Marsh

The reference wetland New River Marsh (site 2, fig. 1) is distant from regional well fields and is unaffected by groundwater withdrawals. New River Marsh (fig. 7A), is about 2.9 acres in size, has a maximum depth of about 3 ft, and exhibits a hydrograph (fig. 7B) typical of natural marshes in the region (Lee and others, 2009). A staff gage was installed in the wetland in 2000 and a shallow wetland well equipped with a recorder was added in May 2001 (Michael Hancock, Southwest Florida Water Management District, unpub. data, 2009). Therefore, the period of record is shorter at this reference wetland than at Green Swamp Cypress and at the well-field wetlands. The period of record at New River Marsh completely overlaps the post-reduction period at the CCWF and the CBRWF wetlands, but only partly overlaps the pre-reduction period at those well fields.

Water reached normal pool in New River Marsh during most years and the wetland was dry for brief periods in some years prior to the beginning of the wet season (fig. 7B). The extent and duration of the flooded area were somewhat similar at New River Marsh during the pre- and post-reduction periods applied to the well field wetlands (fig. 7C), and the wetland increments nearest to the wetland perimeter (41–100 percent) were flooded for longer periods of time at this wetland than the increments nearest the wetland center (fig. 7C). Haag and others (2005) described a similar pattern in a marsh unaffected by groundwater withdrawals (Hillsborough River State Park Marsh). During March 8, 2001, to September 30, 2002, (the part of the record that partly overlaps with the pre-reduction period at the CCWF and CBRWF wetlands) New River Marsh was dry 25 percent of the time (about 17 weeks), 41–80 percent of the wetland was flooded 56 percent of the time, and 81–100 percent of the wetland was flooded 13 percent of the time (about 9 weeks) (fig. 7C, D). Overall, New River Marsh was dry for less time during

Line of sight for survey instruments is greater in marsh wetlands such as New River Marsh than in cypress wetlands.

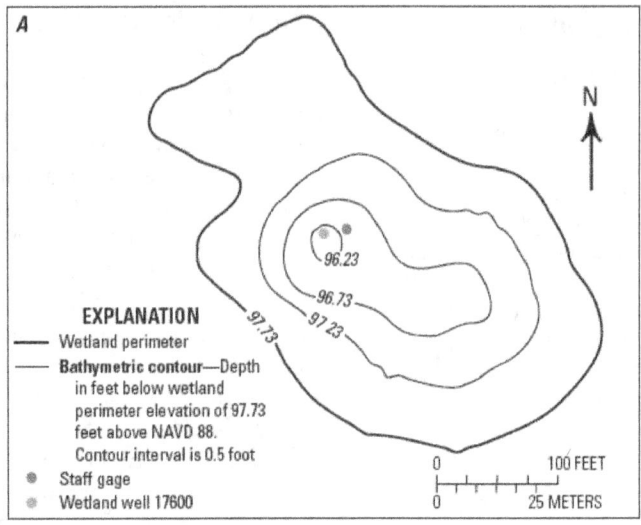

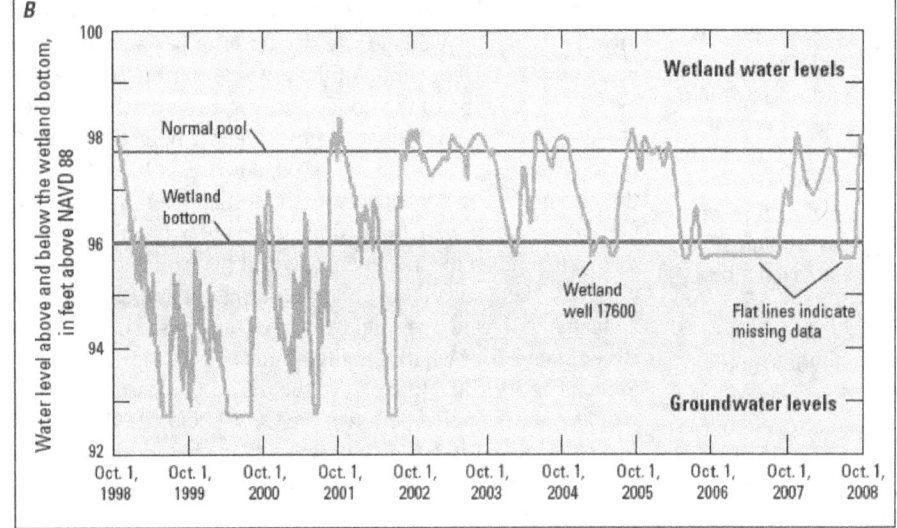

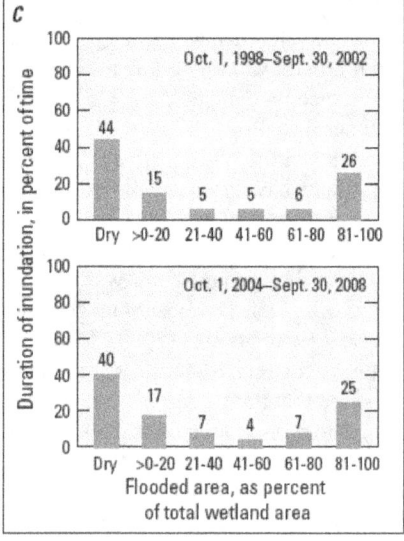

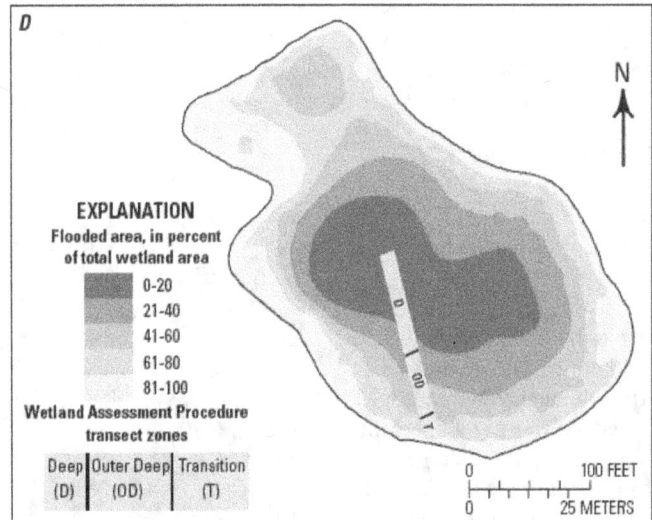

Figure 6.   *A,* Bathymetric map of Green Swamp Cypress in west-central Florida and graphs of *B,* wetland water level and groundwater levels in the wetland monitor well, *C,* the duration of inundation, in percent of time, and *D,* flooded area in percent of total wetland area for Green Swamp Cypress. The symbol > is greater than. Flat lines on hydrograph indicate missing data. NAVD 88 is North American Vertical Datum of 1988.

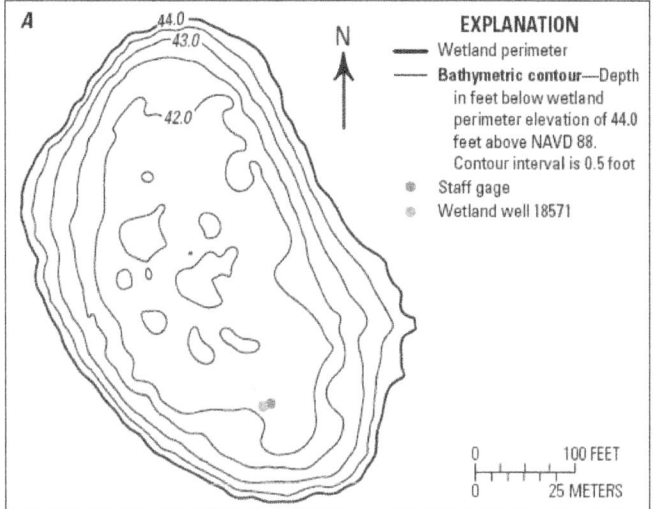

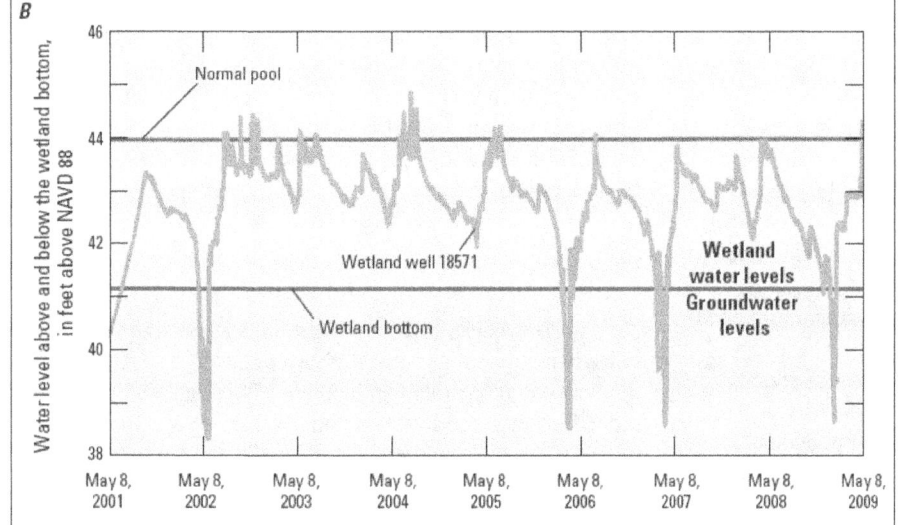

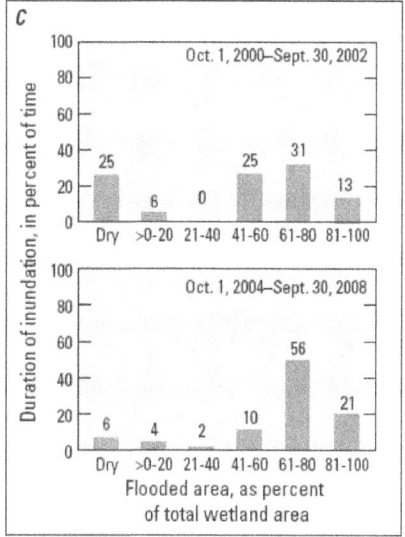

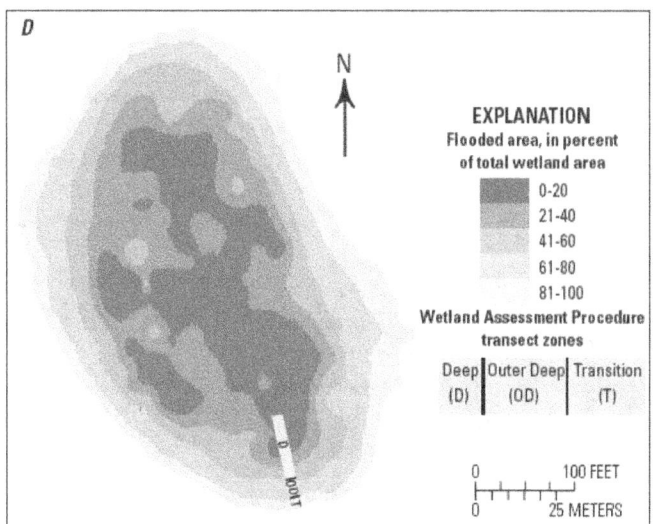

Figure 7. *A,* Bathymetric map of New River Marsh in west-central Florida and graphs of *B,* wetland water level and groundwater levels in the wetland monitor well, *C,* the duration of inundation, in percent of time, and *D,* flooded area in percent of total wetland area for New River Marsh. The symbol > is greater than. NAVD 88 is North American Vertical Datum of 1988.

the post-reduction period (6 percent of the time, or about 12 weeks). About 41–80 percent of the wetland was flooded 66 percent of the time, and 81–100 percent of the wetland was flooded 21 percent of the time (about 44 weeks) (fig. 7C). Compared to Green Swamp Cypress, more of the total area of New River Marsh was flooded for more of the time during both the pre- and post-reduction periods.

Q-1

Q-1 has been affected by groundwater withdrawals, and wetland water levels have not recovered substantially since reductions in groundwater-withdrawal rates began. Q-1, located near the southern boundary of the CBRWF (site 3, fig. 1), is relatively small (about 1.4 acres) and shallow (1.6 ft) (fig. 8A). After the initiation of water-level monitoring in 1990 there was no surface water observed in this wetland through 1998 (Michael Hancock, Southwest Florida Water Management District, unpub. data, 2009), and no surface water was observed during 1999–2002 (fig. 8B).

During the pre-reduction period, Q-1 was dry about 94 percent of the time and up to 20 percent of the wetland area was flooded about 4 percent of the time (about 8 weeks) (fig. 8C, D). The wetland was flooded throughout 81–100 percent of the total area for 2 percent (about 4 weeks) of the pre-reduction period. The wetland was flooded briefly to the elevation of normal pool during 2003–2005 (fig. 8B).

During the post-reduction period, the wetland remained mostly dry (82 percent of the time). The wetland was flooded throughout increments of its total area for short periods (2–4 percent of the time, or about 4–8 weeks), and 81–100 percent of the wetland area was flooded about 4 percent of the time (about 8 weeks). The median elevation of the potentiometric surface of the Upper Floridan aquifer below Q-1 rose about 2 ft during the post-reduction period, but remained about 6 ft below the wetland bottom.

Dry conditions at Q-1.

W-17

Reductions in groundwater-withdrawal rates increased the extent and duration of the flooded area at W-17, which is a relatively large (3.9 acres) and shallow (2.5 ft) wetland (fig. 9A) in the CCWF (site 4, fig. 1). During the pre-reduction period wetland water levels did not reach normal pool, and water rarely was above the bottom of the wetland (fig. 9B). The wetland was dry about 94 percent of the time, and 20 percent or less of the total wetland area was flooded for the remaining 6 percent of the time (about 12 weeks) (fig. 9C, D). Above-average regional rainfall during 2003–2004 (fig. 4) contributed to higher wetland water levels, which reached normal pool during those years (fig. 9B). During the post-reduction period, the wetland was flooded throughout increments of its total area for longer periods of time (3–9 percent, or about 6–19 weeks), and 81–100 percent of the wetland was flooded for 7 percent of the time (about 15 weeks) (fig. 9C). The wetland was dry only 65 percent of the time during the post-reduction period, 29 percent less time than during the pre-reduction period. The median elevation of the potentiometric surface of the upper Floridan aquifer beneath W-17 increased about 8 ft after reductions in groundwater-withdrawal rates (fig. 3), the largest increase of all study wetlands.

W-33

W-33 was less affected by groundwater withdrawals initially compared to other study wetlands in the CCWF, but it also demonstrated an increase in flooded area after reductions in groundwater-withdrawal rates. W-33 is a small (about 1.2 acres), shallow (1.4 ft) wetland (fig. 10A) in the southeastern part of CCWF (site 5, fig. 1). Water levels in this wetland frequently reached normal pool elevation during the past 30 years, and hydroperiods at this site have ranged from 1 to 12 months (Michael Hancock, Southwest Florida Water Management District, unpub. data, 2009). Although water levels were not as affected by groundwater withdrawals as some other sites, this wetland has been affected by three types of disturbances: land management activities, fire, and water deficit. The canopy appears thin because of tree fall and stunted growth of cypress, which may be due to water deficit stress (Michael Hancock, Southwest Florida Water Management District, unpub. data, 2009).

During the pre-reduction period, water levels in W-33 regularly reached normal pool (fig. 10B). The wetland was dry about 40 percent of the time, and 21–40 percent of the wetland was flooded about 14 percent of the time (about 29 weeks) (fig. 10C, D). About 61–80 percent of the wetland was flooded 11 percent of the time (about 23 weeks), and 81–100 percent of the wetland was flooded as much as 30 percent of the time. During the post-reduction period, the wetland was less dry (about 26 percent of the time). The wetland was flooded throughout increments of its total area for slightly longer periods (4–8 percent of the time, or about 8–16 weeks) than before reductions in groundwater-withdrawal rates, and

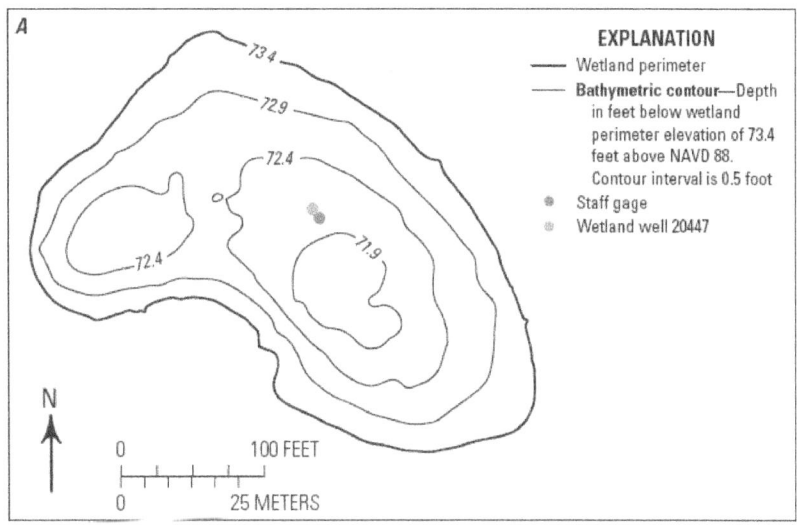

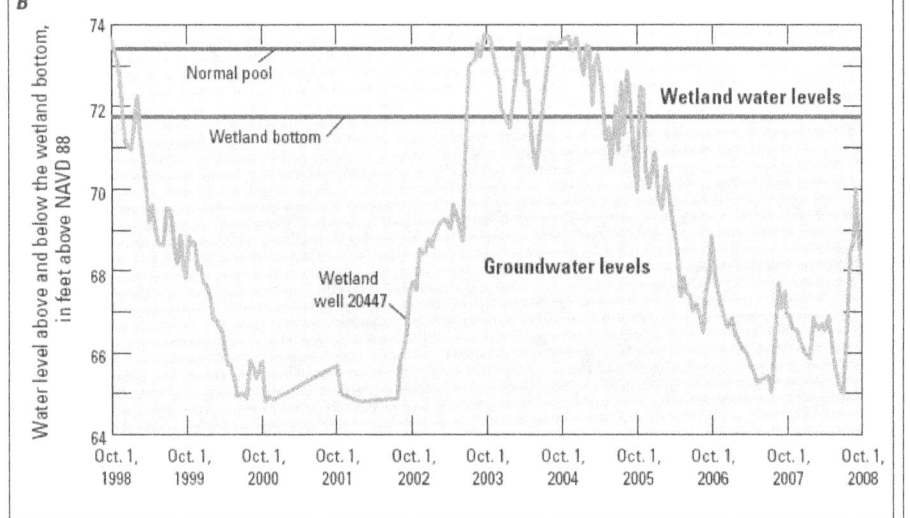

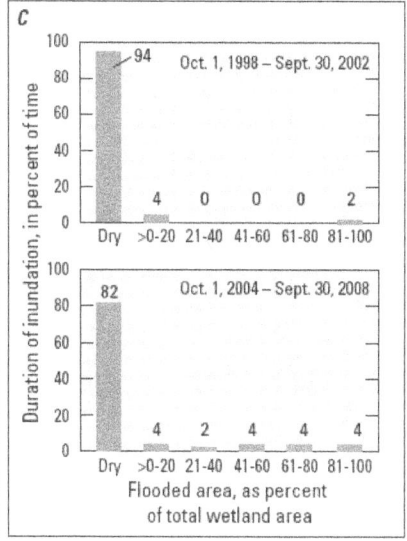

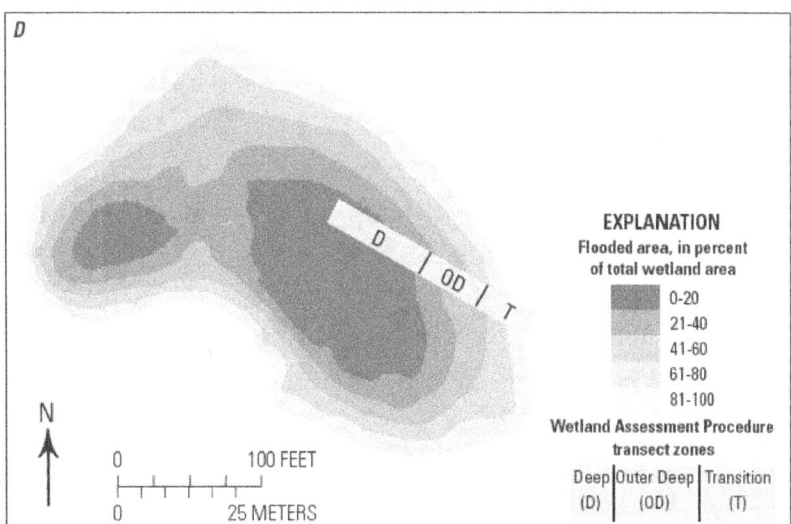

Figure 8. *A,* Bathymetric map of Q-1 in west-central Florida and graphs of *B,* wetland water level and groundwater levels in the wetland monitor well, *C,* the duration of inundation, in percent of time, and *D,* flooded area in percent of total wetland area for Q-1. The symbol > is greater than. NAVD 88 is North American Vertical Datum of 1988.

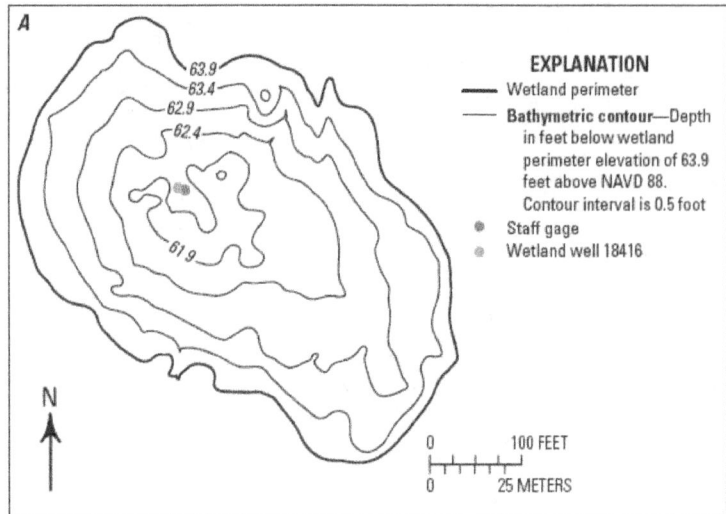

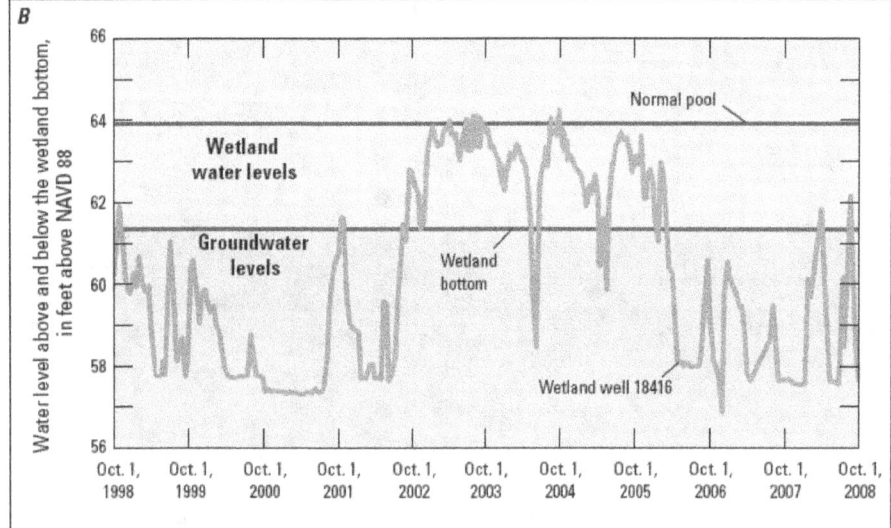

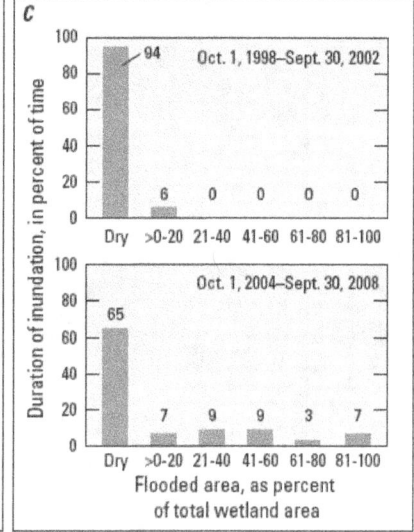

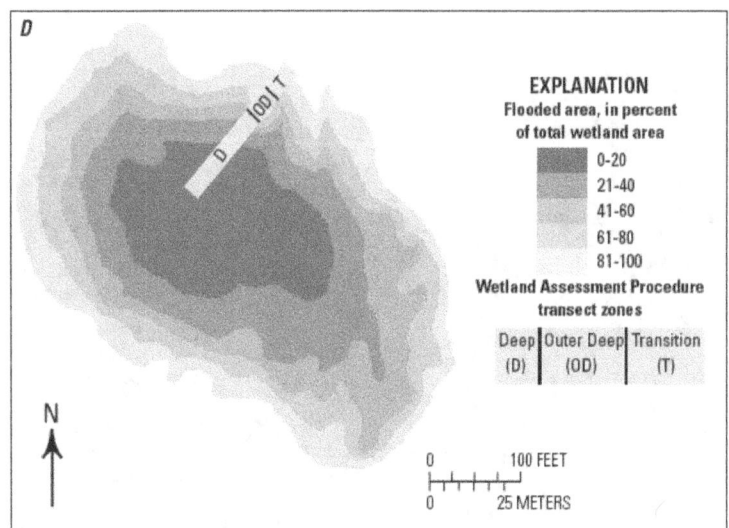

Figure 9. *A,* Bathymetric map of W-17 in west-central Florida and graphs of *B,* wetland water level and groundwater levels in the wetland monitor well, *C,* the duration of inundation, in percent of time, and *D,* flooded area in percent of total wetland area for W-17. The symbol > is greater than. NAVD 88 is North American Vertical Datum of 1988.

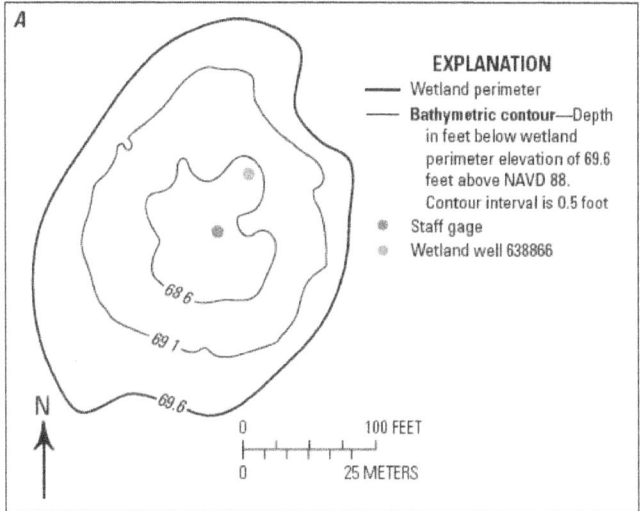

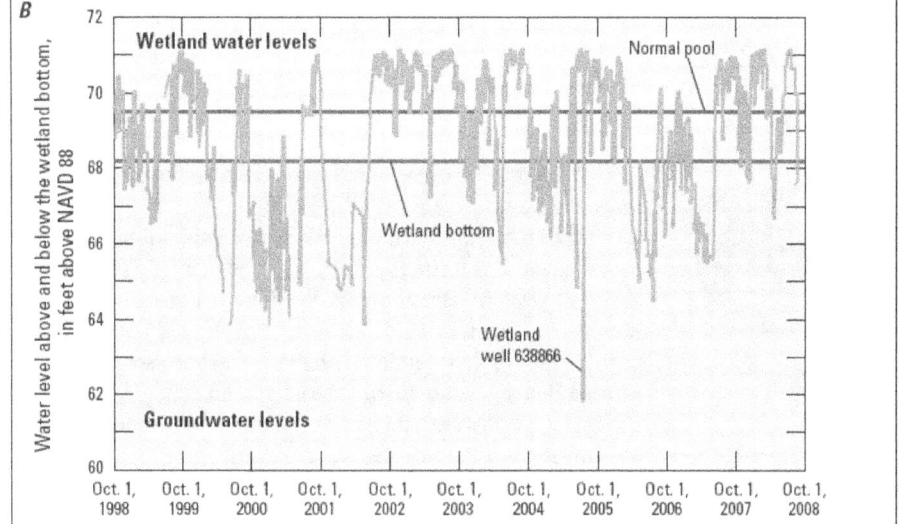

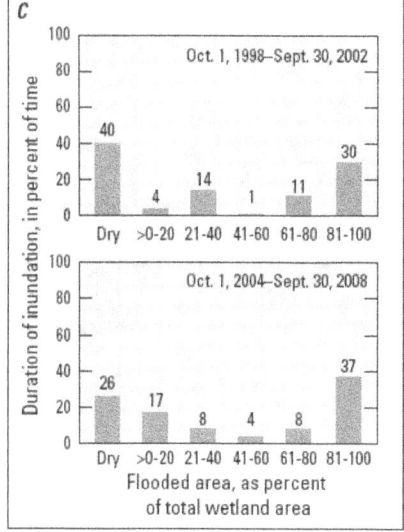

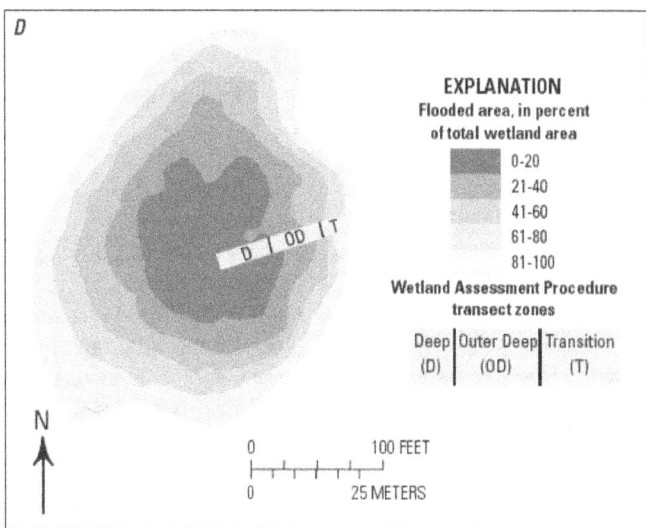

Figure 10. *A,* Bathymetric map of W-33 in west-central Florida and graphs of *B,* wetland water level and groundwater levels in the wetland monitor well, *C,* the duration of inundation, in percent of time, and *D,* flooded area in percent of total wetland area for W-33. The symbol > is greater than. Break in line on hydrograph indicates missing data. NAVD 88 is North American Vertical Datum of 1988.

The interior of W-33 during dry conditions.

was flooded over 81–100 percent of the total wetland area about 37 percent of the time. The median elevation of the potentiometric surface of the Upper Floridan aquifer increased beneath W-33 (fig. 3) by about 3 ft during the post-reduction period, which likely decreased induced leakage from the overlying surficial aquifer and from the wetland. Metz (2011) reported that an increase in the potentiometric surface of the Upper Florida aquifer below wetlands was the primary factor affecting hydrologic recovery of wetlands in well fields.

W-41

Although W-41 was flooded to a greater extent after reductions in groundwater-withdrawal rates, most of the increase in flooded area was confined to less than 20 percent of the total wetland area. W-41 is a relatively large (4.3 acres) isolated wetland with a depth of about 2.7 ft (fig. 11A). W-41 is in the northern part of the CCWF, close to the northern property line (site 6, fig. 1). Since monitoring began in 1981, wetland water levels have been above the wetland bottom only during years of above-average rainfall; otherwise, water levels have averaged 2 to 6 ft below the wetland bottom (Michael Hancock, Southwest Florida Water Management District, unpub. data, 2009). Few physical alterations have

occurred at this wetland other than forest road maintenance. However, overland flow from north of this site that otherwise might contribute water to this wetland can be blocked by the road and the abandoned railroad berm that borders the northern property boundary.

During the pre-reduction period, water flooded the deepest part of W-41 only briefly, late in 1998 (fig. 11B), and the wetland was dry for about 98 percent of the time (fig. 11C, D). Up to 20 percent of the wetland was flooded for 2 percent of the pre-reduction period (about 4 weeks). During the post-reduction period up to 20 percent of the wetland was flooded 15 percent of the time (about 31 weeks), and 81–100 percent of the wetland was flooded about 6 percent of the time (about 12 weeks) (fig. 11C). The wetland was dry about 75 percent of the time during the post-reduction period, a 23 percent decrease from the pre-reduction period. After reductions in groundwater-withdrawal rates, the median elevation of the potentiometric surface of the Upper Floridan aquifer increased about 5 ft beneath W-41 (fig. 3).

W-56

W-56 was less dry after reductions in groundwater-withdrawal rates and the deepest parts of the wetland were flooded for more than three times as long. W-56 is a small (about 0.7 acre) and shallow (1.6 ft) dome-shaped cypress wetland (fig. 12A) in the southwestern part of the CCWF (site 7, fig. 1). Hydrologic monitoring began in 1978, and water levels seldom reach normal pool in this wetland (Michael Hancock, Southwest Florida Water Management District, unpub. data, 2009). The small size of this wetland makes it particularly responsive to the effects of below-average rainfall because the smaller storage capacity allows it to dry out more quickly (Metz, 2011). Few alterations have occurred at this wetland since monitoring began other than controlled burns of adjacent saw palmetto (Michael Hancock, Southwest Florida Water Management District, unpub. data, 2009).

During the pre-reduction period water levels in W-56 were below the wetland bottom for much of 1999–2001 (fig. 12B), and the wetland was dry about 75 percent of the time (fig. 12C). Up to 20 percent of the wetland was flooded for 6 percent of the time (about 12 weeks), and 61–100 percent of the wetland was flooded for 13 percent of the time (about 27 weeks) (fig. 12C, D). During above-average regional rainfall (2003–2004) and under conditions of reduced groundwater-withdrawal rates after 2002, water levels reached normal pool in W-56 (fig. 12B). During the post-reduction period the wetland was dry for 56 percent of the time, and up to 20 percent of the wetland was flooded for 27 percent of the time. The flooded area extended throughout 61–100 percent of the wetland for about 12 percent of the time (about 25 weeks), an extent and duration similar to the pre-reduction period (fig. 12C). The median elevation of the potentiometric surface of the Upper Florida aquifer beneath W-56 increased about 4 ft in the post-reduction period compared to the pre-reduction period (fig. 3).

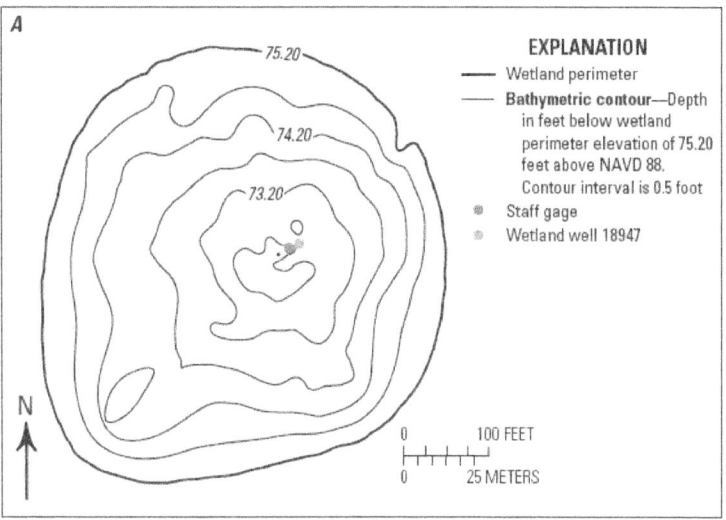

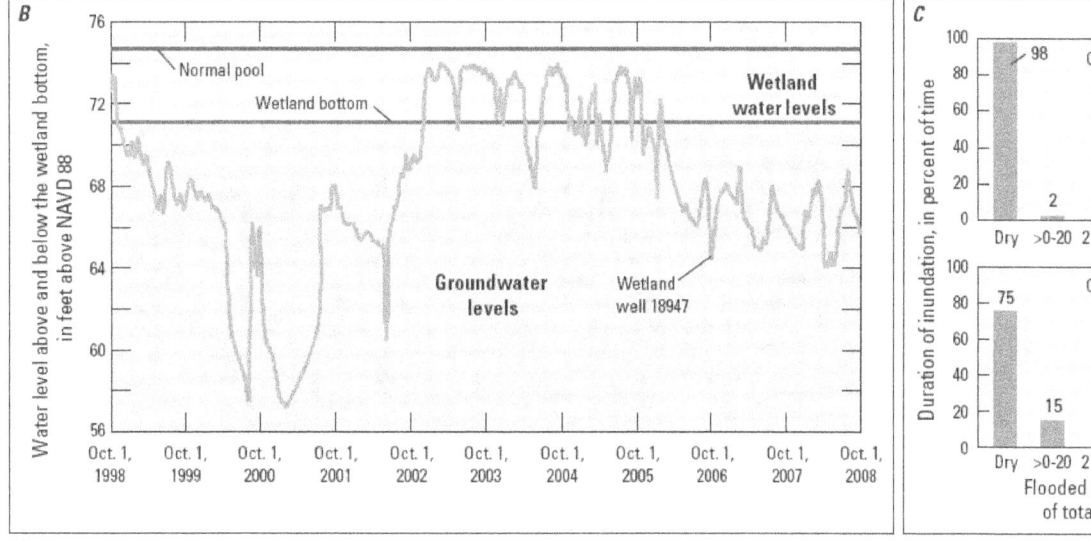

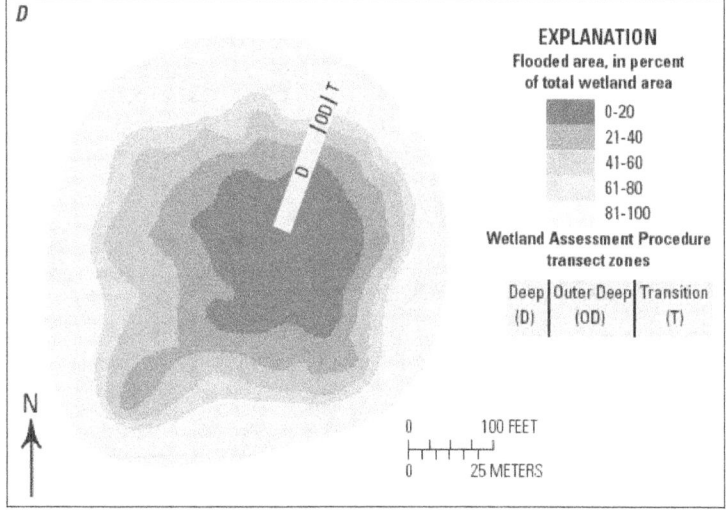

Figure 11. *A,* Bathymetric map of W-41 in west-central Florida and graphs of *B,* wetland water level and groundwater levels in the wetland monitor well, *C,* the duration of inundation, in percent of time, and *D,* flooded area in percent of total wetland area for W-41. The symbol > is greater than. NAVD 88 is North American Vertical Datum of 1988.

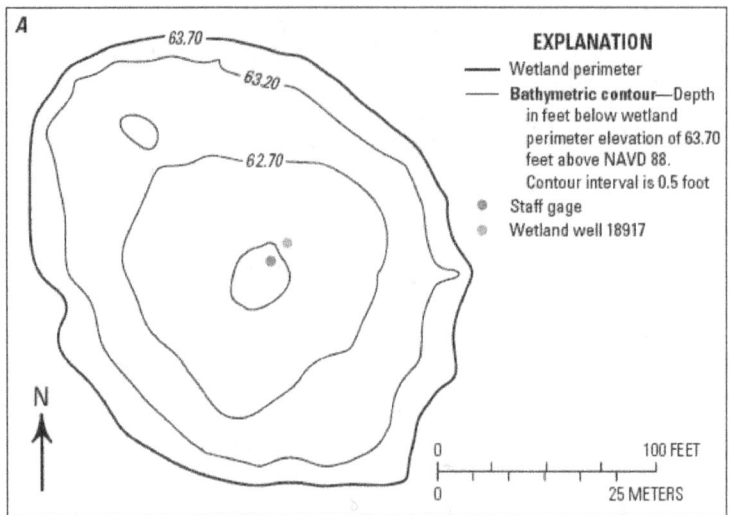

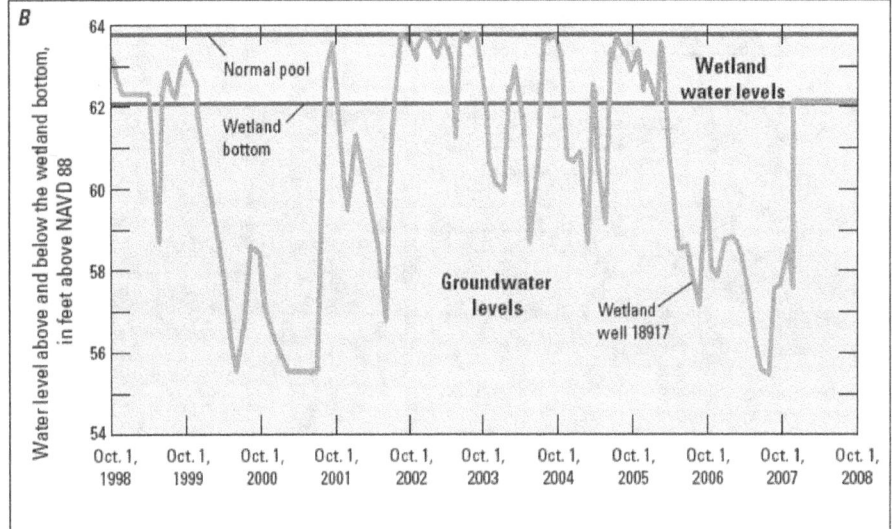

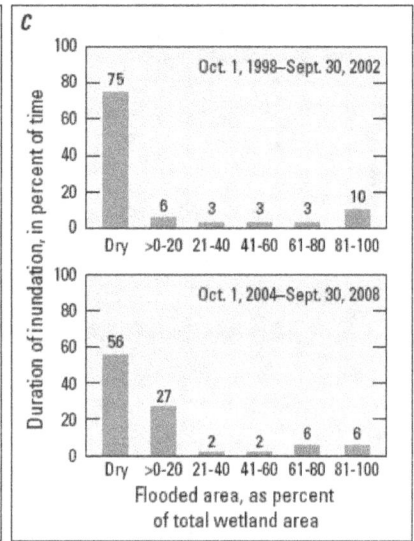

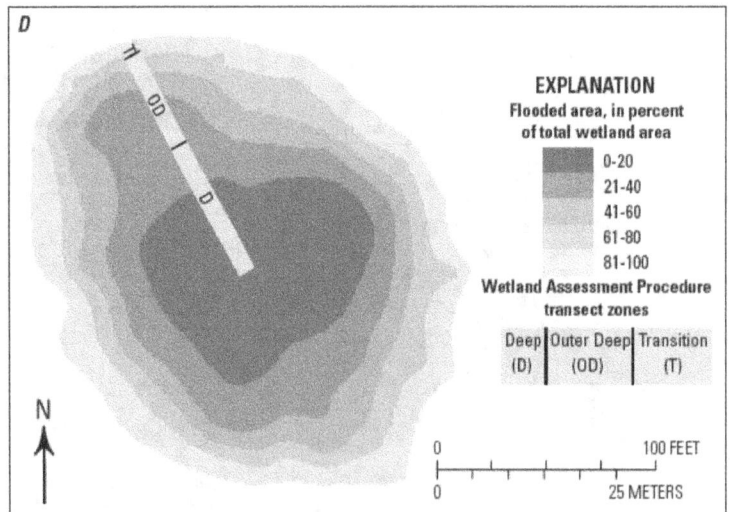

Figure 12.   *A,* Bathymetric map of W-56 in west-central Florida and graphs of *B,* wetland water level and groundwater levels in the wetland monitor well, *C,* the duration of inundation, in percent of time, and *D,* flooded area in percent of total wetland area for W-56. The symbol > is greater than. NAVD 88 is North American Vertical Datum of 1988.

Starkey D

The extent and duration of the flooded area were mostly unchanged at Starkey D when the pre- and post-reduction periods were compared. Starkey D (site 8, fig. 1), in the western part of the SWF, is a large (5.3 acres) wetland with a maximum depth of about 4.7 ft (fig. 13*A*). Although Starkey D had considerable standing water in 1975, the wetland has been drier in subsequent years and no standing water was observed during some years (Michael Hancock, Southwest Florida Water Management District, unpub. data, 2009). This is not typical for natural cypress wetlands, which have some standing water even in relatively dry years. For example, Lee and others (2009) reported that natural cypress wetlands in the northern Tampa Bay region were dry about 40 percent of the year and were flooded throughout at least a part of the wetland area for about 60 percent of the year. An area of severe soil subsidence has been identified in the western part of Starkey D. Sinkhole activity and the prolonged absence of surface water in the wetland can contribute to subsidence.

During the pre-reduction period Starkey D was dry 81 percent of the time. About 81–100 percent of the wetland was flooded about 10 percent of the time, but most increments of the total wetland area were rarely flooded (fig. 13*C*, *D*). When rainfall was above average during 2004, water was sometimes 1–2 ft above the wetland bottom at the staff gage (fig. 13*B*). During the post-reduction period the wetland was dry 83 percent of the time and up to 20 percent of the total wetland area was flooded about 7 percent of the time (about 15 weeks). The remaining increments of the wetland area were seldom flooded (fig. 13*C*). Although reductions in groundwater-withdrawal rates at the SWF were initiated in December 2007, the median elevation of the potentiometric surface of the Upper Floridan aquifer did not increase significantly beneath Starkey D during the post-reduction period (fig. 3).

The extent and duration of the flooded area at Starkey D most likely did not increase during the post-reduction period because the elevation of the potentiometric surface of the Upper Floridan aquifer did not increase, and subsidence or sinkhole activity facilitated continued downward leakage. In a study of factors known to influence the hydrologic condition of wetlands, Metz (2011) reported that karst features below or near wetlands, subsidence, and high permeability sediments underlying wetlands impeded the ability of these wetlands to recover when groundwater-withdrawal rates were reduced. Metz (2011) also reported that wetlands isolated from surface-water connections to near-by water sources, such as other wetlands, streams, and ponds, were less likely to recover after groundwater-withdrawal rates were reduced.

Starkey E

The extent and duration of the flooded area at Starkey E did not increase when the pre- and post-reduction periods were compared. Starkey E is a deep (about 11.9 ft) marsh with a surface area of about 3.4 acres (fig. 14*A*) in the western part of the SWF about 1 mi from the western boundary (site 9, fig. 1). High water levels in the summer of 1975 failed to flood much of the marsh fringe, and low water levels have continued over the years, allowing sand pine (*Pinus clausa*) to invade the marsh fringe (Michael Hancock, Southwest Florida Water Management District, unpub. data, 2009). Staff gage records from the late 1970s through the mid-1980s indicate that peak summertime water levels declined during the period.

Starkey E is the deepest wetland in the study (fig. 14*A*) and a large volume of water (more than 15 acre-feet (acre-ft; app. 10) is needed to flood the wetland to the perimeter. Although water levels at Starkey E did not reach normal pool (fig. 14*B*) during the study period, the wetland never was completely dry and always held water in a small pool in the center. During the pre-reduction period less than 20 percent of the wetland was flooded about half (52 percent) of the time, 21–40 percent of the wetland was flooded about 26 percent of the time, and 41–60 percent of the wetland was flooded

Dry conditions and encroachment of pines at Starkey D.

Starkey E, a large deep marsh.

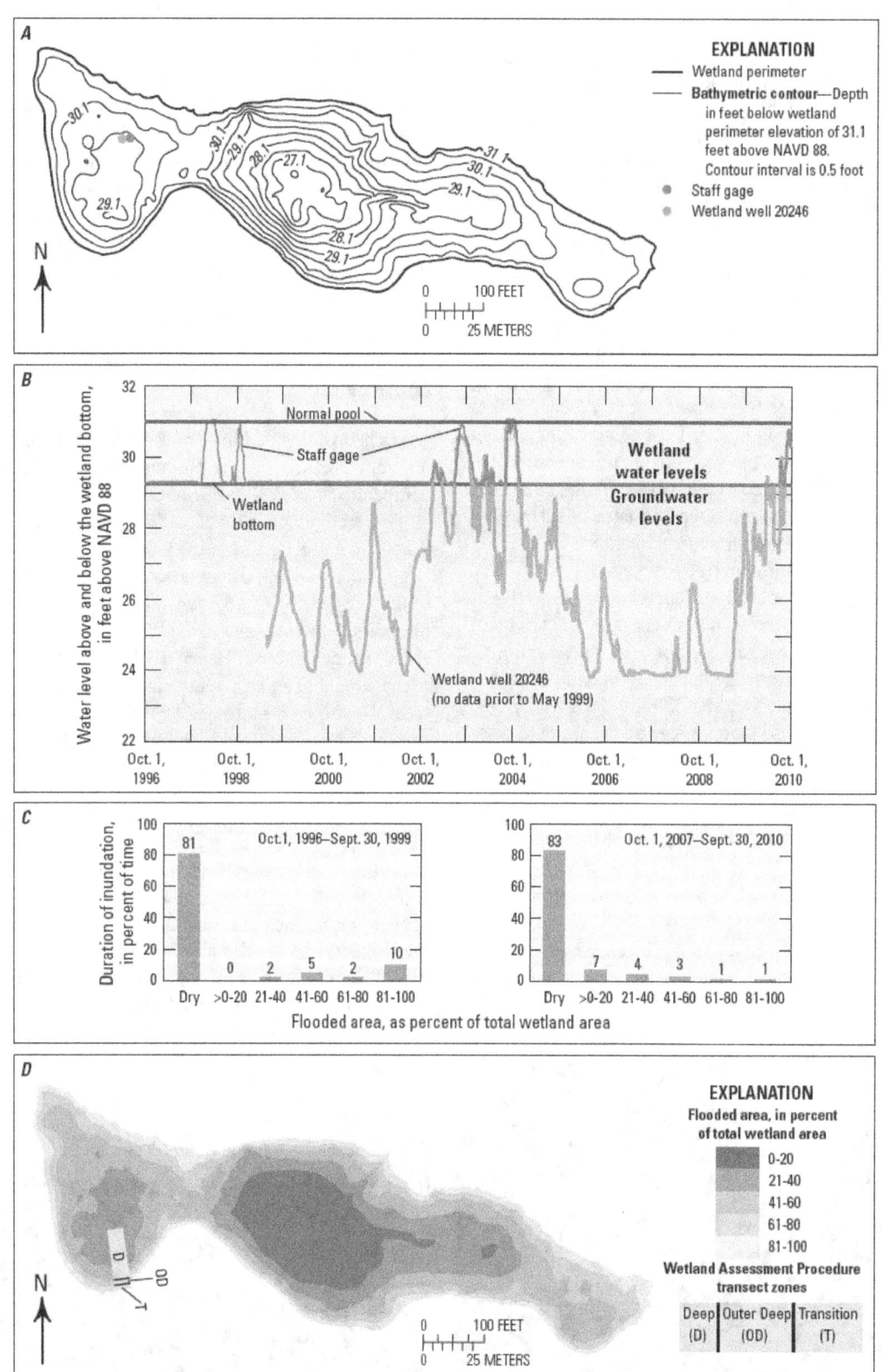

Figure 13. *A,* Bathymetric map of Starkey D in west-central Florida and graphs of *B,* wetland water level and groundwater levels in the wetland monitor well, *C,* the duration of inundation, in percent of time, and *D,* flooded area in percent of total wetland area for Starkey D. The symbol > is greater than. Flat lines on hydrograph indicate missing data. NAVD 88 is North American Vertical Datum of 1988.

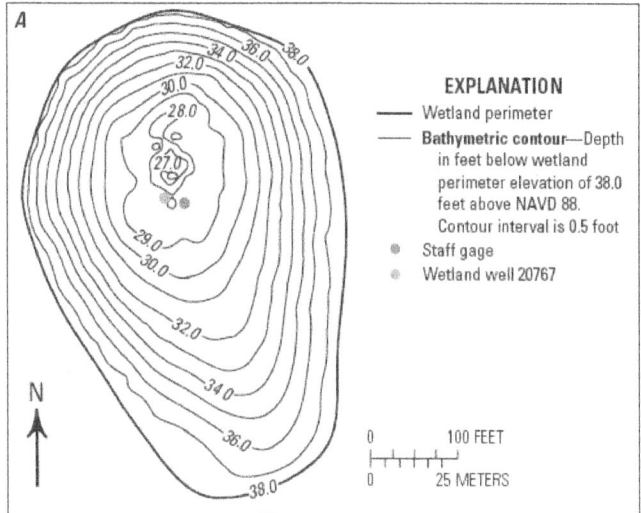

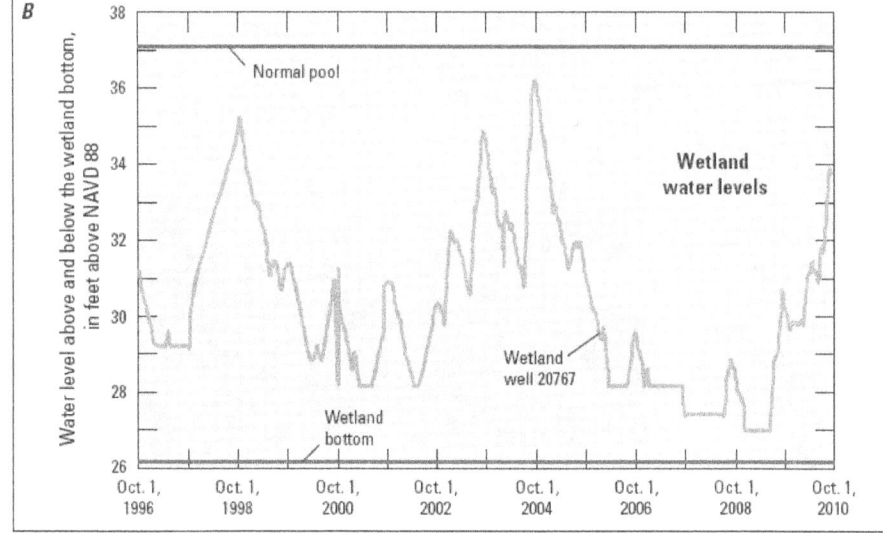

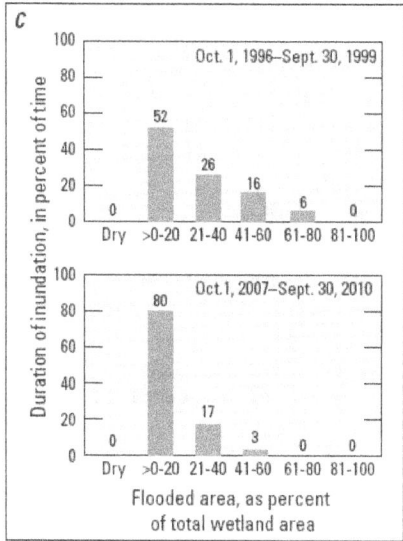

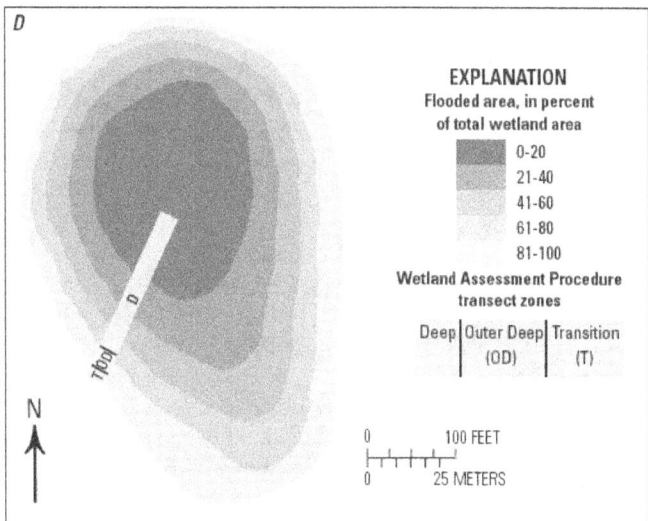

Figure 14. *A,* Bathymetric map of Starkey E in west-central Florida and graphs of *B,* wetland water level and groundwater levels in the wetland monitor well, *C,* the duration of inundation, in percent of time, and *D,* flooded area in percent of total wetland area for Starkey E. The symbol > is greater than. Flat line segments on hydrograph indicate missing data. NAVD 88 is North American Vertical Datum of 1988.

16 percent of the time (about 25 weeks) (fig. 14C, D). During the post-reduction period, less than 20 percent of the total area was flooded about 80 percent of the time. About 21–40 percent of the total area was flooded only 17 percent of the time (about 28 weeks), and 41–60 percent of the wetland was rarely flooded (3 percent of the time, or about 5 weeks). The median elevation of the potentiometric surface of the Upper Floridan aquifer beneath Starkey E did not change substantially during the post-reduction period compared to the pre-reduction period (fig. 3). The flooded area at Starkey E most likely did not increase because the elevation of the potentiometric surface of the Upper Floridan aquifer did not increase, and subsidence or sinkhole activity facilitated continued downward leakage from the wetland.

Starkey N

Starkey N was dry for less time during the post-reduction period and the wetland was flooded to the perimeter for longer periods of time after reductions in groundwater-withdrawal rates. Starkey N is a relatively large (3.9 acres) shallow (1.6 ft) wetland (fig. 15A) in the far eastern part of the SWF (site 10, fig. 1), and the wetland was flooded in the deepest part for a few weeks each year during the entire period of record (fig. 15B).

During the pre-reduction period Starkey N was dry about 57 percent of the time, and 81–100 percent of the wetland was flooded for 22 percent of the time (about 46 weeks) (fig. 15C, D). During the post-reduction period the wetland was dry for about 31 percent of the time, 61–80 percent of the wetland was flooded for 10 percent of the time (about 21 weeks), and 81–100 percent of the wetland was flooded for 53 percent of the time (fig. 15C), more than twice as much time compared to the pre-reduction period. The median elevation of the potentiometric surface of the Upper Floridan aquifer beneath Starkey N increased about 4 ft during the post-reduction period (fig. 3), and reductions in groundwater-withdrawal rates likely reduced induced leakage from the surficial aquifer and contributed to the greater extent and duration of the flooded area at this site.

Starkey 108

The extent and duration of the flooded area increased at Starkey 108 after reductions in groundwater-withdrawal rates. Starkey 108 is a small (about 1.1 acres) shallow (1.7 ft) wetland (fig. 16A) in the eastern part of the SWF (site 11, fig. 1). Water levels in Starkey 108 from the late 1980s through the 1990s were lower than water levels in wetlands unaffected by groundwater withdrawals (Michael Hancock, Southwest Florida Water Management District, unpub. data, 2009).

Water levels in Starkey 108 were seldom above the wetland bottom during the pre-reduction period (fig. 16B). The wetland was dry about 72 percent of the time and most increments of the wetland area were flooded only 1–3 percent of the time (about 2–6 weeks) (fig 16C, D). About

81–100 percent of the total wetland area was flooded for about 21 percent of the time (about 44 weeks), and the wetland hydrograph (16B) indicates that this likely occurred during the winter of 1997 and early spring of 1998, an interval of above average rainfall recorded at the Tarpon Springs rainfall station. During the post-reduction period, the wetland was dry for 44 percent of the time, or 38 percent less time than during the pre-reduction period. The wetland was flooded throughout much of its total area for longer periods of time, and 61–100 percent of the total wetland area was flooded for 39 percent of the time during the post-reduction period. The median elevation of the potentiometric surface of the Upper Floridan aquifer beneath Starkey 108 increased about 4 ft during the post-reduction period compared to the pre-reduction period (fig. 3).

Cypress trees in Starkey 108.

Flooded Area Summary

Flooded area, expressed as a percentage of the total wetland area, was quantified at two reference wetlands and nine wetlands in well fields during periods before and after groundwater-withdrawal rates were reduced. Four-year pre-reduction (October 1998–September 2002) and post-reduction (October 2004–September 2008) periods were applied to wetlands in the CCWF and CBRWF. Three-year pre-reduction (October 1996–September 1999) and post-reduction (October 2007–September 2010) periods were applied to wetlands in the SWF. Total rainfall amounts were similar (differed by 1 percent or less) during the respective pre- and post-reduction periods, which reduced the effect that rainfall variability had on the analysis. The data describing flooded area of well-field wetlands in the pre- and post-reduction periods were used to average-out the effects of year-to-year rainfall differences in an effort to reveal the effects of reduced groundwater-withdrawal rates. The groundwater-withdrawal rates in the post-reduction period at the CCWF, CBRWF, and SWF were 30, 24, and 64 percent less than the pre-reduction rates, respectively.

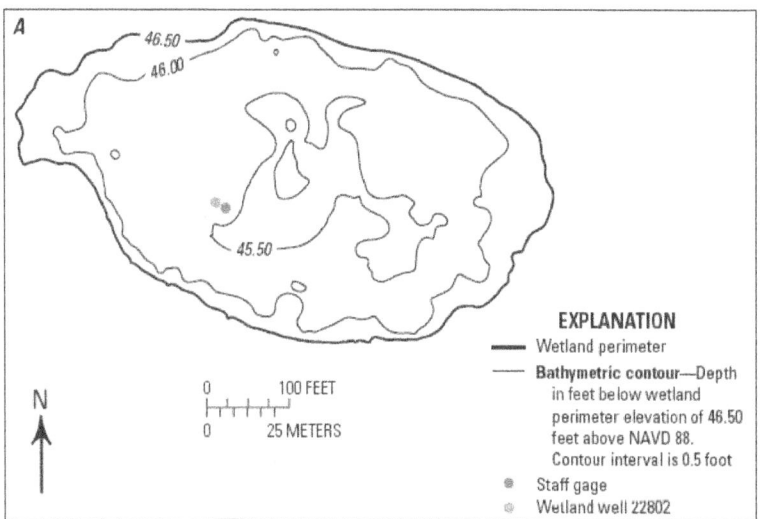

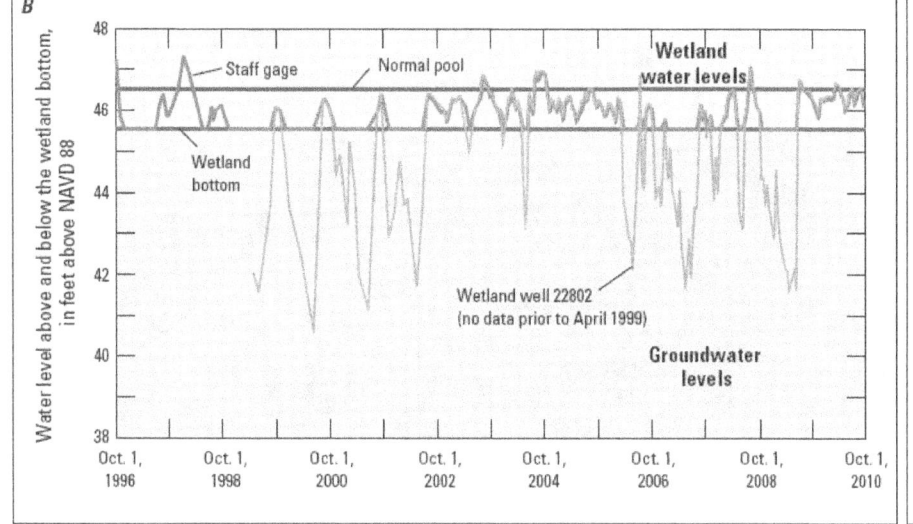

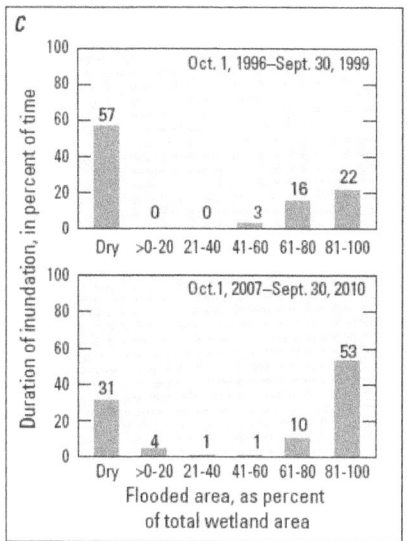

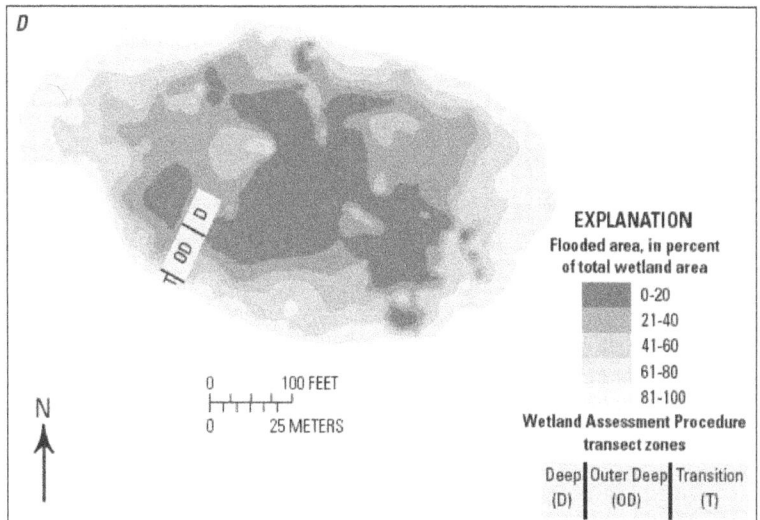

Figure 15.   *A,* Bathymetric map of Starkey N in west-central Florida and graphs of *B,* wetland water level and groundwater levels in the wetland monitor well, *C,* the duration of inundation, in percent of time, and *D,* flooded area in percent of total wetland area for Starkey N. The symbol > is greater than. NAVD 88 is North American Vertical Datum of 1988.

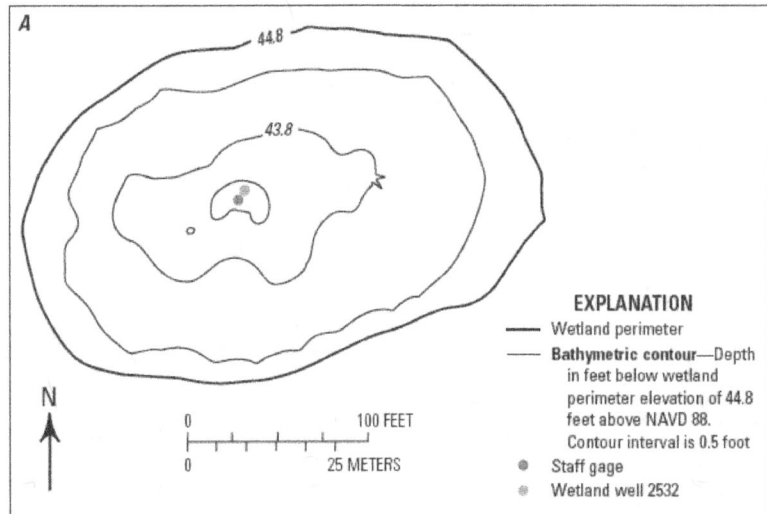

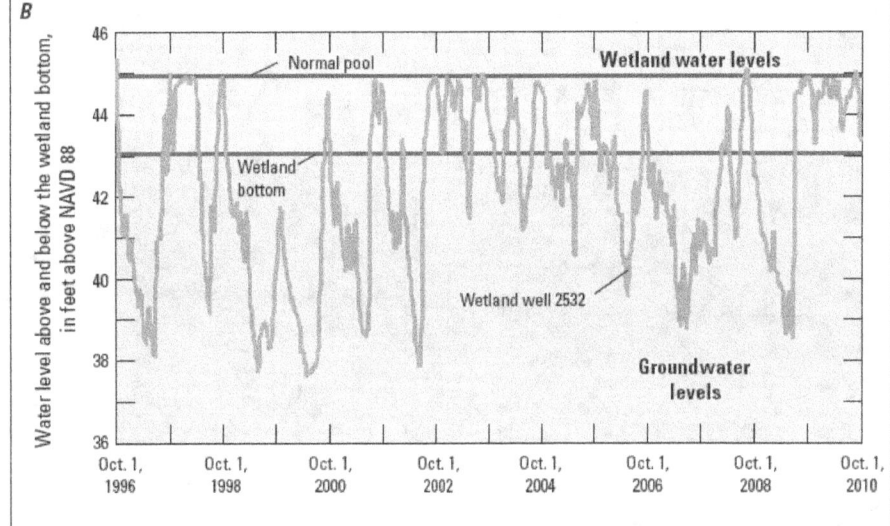

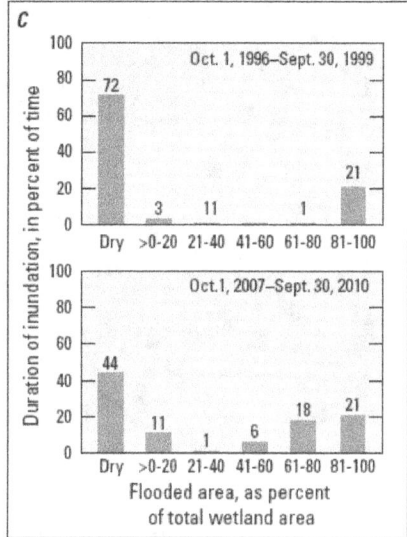

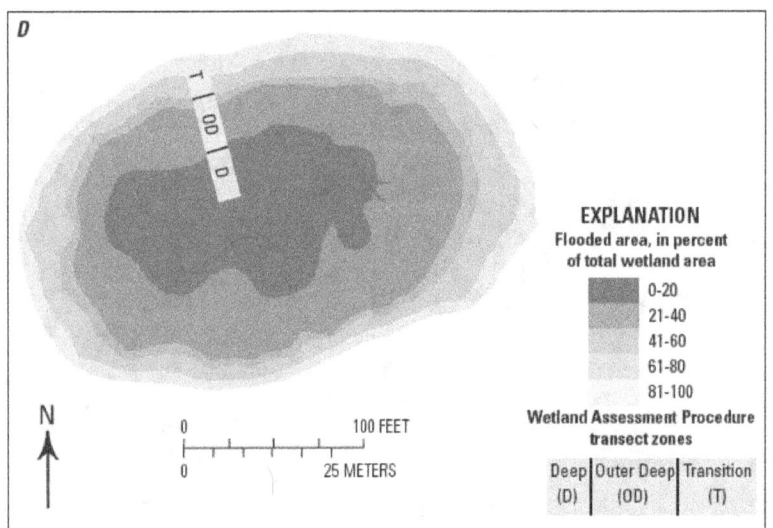

Figure 16. *A,* Bathymetric map of Starkey 108 in west-central Florida and graphs of *B,* wetland water level and groundwater levels in the wetland monitor well, *C,* the duration of inundation, in percent of time, and *D,* flooded area in percent of total wetland area for Starkey 108. The symbol > is greater than. NAVD 88 is North American Vertical Datum of 1988.

The extent and duration of the flooded area at the Green Swamp Cypress reference wetland were similar during the pre- and post-reduction periods applied to wetlands at CCWF and CBRWF, indicating that short-term variability in rainfall did not affect longer-term flooded area frequencies at this unimpacted wetland. The extent and duration of the flooded area were somewhat similar at the New River Marsh reference wetland during the pre-and post-reduction periods, but the period of record at this site did not overlap the entire pre-reduction period. Compared to Green Swamp Cypress, more of the total area of New River Marsh was flooded for more of the time during both the pre- and post-reduction periods.

One of the five wetlands in the CCWF and CBRWF (W-33) had the extent and duration of flooded area similar to that observed at the reference wetlands both before and after reductions in groundwater-withdrawal rates. Water levels in W-33 reached normal pool during both the pre-reduction and post-reduction periods. The median elevation of the potentiometric surface of the Upper Floridan aquifer also increased beneath W-33 by about 4 ft during the post-reduction period, which likely decreased leakage from the surficial aquifer and from the wetland.

The other four wetlands in the CCWF and CBRWF were mostly dry before reductions in groundwater-withdrawal rates; that is, less than 20 percent of the total wetland area was flooded for at least 75 percent of the time. Two of those four wetlands in the CCWF (W-56 and W-17) had increases in flooded-area extent and duration after reductions in groundwater-withdrawal rates, and were dry for substantially less time than during the pre-reduction period. The median elevation of the potentiometric surface of the Upper Floridan aquifer was about 4–7 ft higher beneath these two wetlands during the period after reductions in groundwater-withdrawal rates, when the pre- and post-reduction periods were compared, and this was the primary cause of increases in flooded area.

The other two wetlands (W-41 and Q-1) recovered slightly but remained mostly dry after reductions in groundwater-withdrawal rates. W-41 was dry 23 percent less time in the post-reduction period, but most of the increase in flooded area was confined to less than 20 percent of the total wetland area. The median elevation of the potentiometric surface of the Upper Floridan aquifer increased beneath W-41 by about 5 ft after reductions in groundwater-withdrawal rates but was still about 9 ft below the wetland bottom. Q-1 was dry for about 12 percent less time in the post-reduction period, when the pre- and post-reduction periods were compared. The median elevation of the potentiometric surface of the Upper Floridan aquifer increased beneath Q-1 by about 2 ft after reductions in groundwater-withdrawal rates, but remained 6 ft below the wetland bottom. Other factors, including karst features below or near the wetland bottom, high permeability sediments underlying the wetland, and topographic isolation from other surface waters could contribute to the lack of recovery of water levels in these wetlands (Metz, 2011).

Two of the four study wetlands at the SWF had flooded areas that increased in extent and duration during the post-reduction period, when the pre- and post-reduction periods were compared. Starkey N was dry for 45 percent less time

and increments of the total wetland area were flooded for more than twice as much time after reductions in groundwater-withdrawal rates. Starkey 108 was dry for about 38 percent less time after reductions, and increments of the total wetland area were flooded for longer periods of time during the post-reduction period. The median elevation of the potentiometric surface of the Upper Floridan aquifer increased beneath both Starkey N and Starkey 108 by about 4 ft after reductions in groundwater-withdrawal rates and this was the primary cause of increases in flooded area.

The other two wetlands in the SWF did not experience an increase in the extent or duration of the flooded area after reductions in groundwater-withdrawal rates. Patterns of inundation were unchanged at Starkey D when the pre- and post-reduction periods were compared, and the wetland remained mostly dry. At Starkey E, the extent and duration of the flooded area decreased during the post-reduction period. The median elevation of the potentiometric surface of the Upper Floridan aquifer did not increase beneath Starkey D and Starkey E during the post-reduction period, and downward leakage from these wetlands was therefore not diminished.

Description of Plant Zonation Following Reductions in Groundwater-Withdrawal Rates

Vegetation patterns described in this study were determined using the WAP surveys completed during 2005–2010. The distribution of vegetation for each of the study wetlands was interpreted with reference to the extent and duration of the flooded area for the post-reduction periods presented already.

Green Swamp Cypress

In the Green Swamp Cypress reference site pond cypress (*Taxodium ascendens*) is the dominant tree species and buttonbush (*Cephalanthus occidentalis*) is found in deeper parts of the wetland (Rochow and Lopez, 1984). Woody species include dahoon (*Ilex cassine*) and fetterbush (*Lyonia lucida*), whereas common herbaceous species include Virginia chainfern (*Woodwardia virginica*), lesser creeping rush (*Juncus repens*), and taperleaf waterhorehound (*Lycopus rubellus*).

The WAP scores for Green Swamp Cypress were 5 for groundcover, 5 for shrubs, and 5 for trees (table 4). These scores are indicative of a cypress wetland that has water levels in the expected range for unimpacted wetlands in west-central Florida. The Deep zone is flooded when about 40 percent of the wetland is flooded (fig. 6D). Groundcover species were almost entirely OBL or FACW, and weighted-average scores for groundcover species were between 3.2 and 5.0 (table 5). The weighted-average score for shrubs varied from 3.0–5.0, and for trees was 5.0. The high scores reflect the favorable water-level conditions in this wetland, which is unaffected by any groundwater withdrawals.

Table 4.   Wetland Assessment Procedure scores for study wetlands in west-central Florida.

[na, not enough plant cover to make evaluation]

Wetland name	Well Field	Year	Groundcover	Shrub	Tree
Green Swamp Cypress	reference	2005	5	5	5
		2006	5	5	5
		2007	3	5	5
		2008	5	5	5
		2009	5	5	5
		2010	5	5	5
New River Marsh	reference	2005	3	3	3
		2006	5	4	4
		2007	4	3	3
		2008	4	3	4
		2009	4	4	3
		2010	4	4	3
Q-1	Cross Bar Ranch Well Field	2005	3	3	5
		2006	3	2	3
		2007	2	3	3
		2008	2	2	3
W-17	Cypress Creek Well Field	2005	3	3	3
		2006	3	3	3
		2007	3	4	3
		2008	3	na	3
W-33	Cypress Creek Well Field	2005	4	5	5
		2006	3	5	5
		2007	3	5	5
		2008	4	5	5
W-41	Cypress Creek Well Field	2005	2	2	2
		2006	3	3	2
		2007	2	na	2
		2008	2	2	2
W-56	Cypress Creek Well Field	2005	3	4	4
		2006	4	4	4
		2007	3	5	4
		2008	3	5	4
Starkey D	Starkey Well Field	2005	2	2	2
		2006	2	2	2
		2007	2	2	2
		2008	3	2	2
		2009	3	2	2
		2010	3	2	2
Starkey E	Starkey Well Field	2005	2	2	2
		2006	2	2	2
		2007	2	2	2
		2008	2	2	2
		2009	2	2	2
		2010	3	1	1
Starkey N	Starkey Well Field	2005	4	5	5
		2006	4	5	5
		2007	3	5	5
		2008	4	5	5
		2009	4	5	5
		2010	4	5	5
Starkey 108	Starkey Well Field	2005	3	5	4
		2006	3	5	4
		2007	3	5	4
		2008	4	na	5
		2009	3	5	5
		2010	4	5	5

Table 5. Weighted average scores in Wetland Assessment Procedure zones for study wetlands in west-central Florida.

[WAP, Wetland Assessment Procedure; D, deep zone; OD, outer deep zone; T, transition zone; na, not enough cover to make evaluation]

Wetland Name	Year	Groundcover			Shrubs			Trees		
		D	OD	T	D	OD	T	D	OD	T
Green Swamp Cypress	2005	5.0	4.0	4.0	na	na	3.0	5.0	5.0	5.0
	2006	na	4.0	5.0	5.0	na	4.7	5.0	5.0	5.0
	2007	3.2	4.0	4.0	na	na	na	5.0	5.0	na
	2008	5.0	4.0	3.6	5.0	5.0	4.0	5.0	5.0	5.0
New River Marsh	2005	5.0	4.2	na	na	2.0	na	na	na	na
	2006	5.0	4.0	na	na	2.0	na	na	2.0	na
	2007	4.9	4.1	na	na	2.0	na	na	na	na
	2008	4.9	4.1	na	2.0	2.0	na	2.0	2.0	na
Q-1	2005	3.9	3.2	4.0	4.4	2.8	3.5	5.0	5.0	5.0
	2006	3.8	3.8	na	4.3	3.0	3.5	5.0	5.0	5.0
	2007	2.6	3.0	1.0	3.6	3.2	3.5	5.0	5.0	na
	2008	2.5	2.1	4.0	3.3	2.5	2.1	4.9	5.0	5.0
W-17	2005	4.5	3.5	2.7	3.0	3.3	3.7	4.9	4.2	3.0
	2006	4.1	3.4	2.1	3.0	2.5	2.5	4.9	4.2	3.0
	2007	3.8	2.1	2.0	3.0	2.5	3.0	4.5	3.4	2.3
	2008	3.2	1.0	1.0	na	na	na	na	na	na
W-33	2005	4.5	4.1	4.0	5.0	na	3.0	5.0	5.0	5.0
	2006	4.1	3.7	3.4	5.0	na	2.0	5.0	5.0	5.0
	2007	4.3	4.0	3.6	5.0	5.0	1.5	5.0	5.0	4.0
	2008	4.3	3.9	3.7	5.0	5.0	3.5	4.9	5.0	5.0
W-41	2005	2.3	2.4	2.2	3.2	1.0	3.0	4.1	3.0	3.0
	2006	3.8	2.4	2.2	3.3	1.0	1.3	4.4	3.0	3.0
	2007	2.6	2.3	2.8	2.5	1.0	1.3	4.3	3.0	3.0
	2008	1.5	na	na	na	na	na	na	na	na
W-56	2005	4.0	4.5	na	na	4.0	na	4.8	4.3	na
	2006	4.0	4.5	na	na	5.0	na	5.0	4.9	na
	2007	4.0	4.2	na	na	na	na	5.0	4.9	na
	2008	4.5	na	na	na	na	na	na	na	na
Starkey D	2005	4.0	1.0	na	2.0	na	na	4.6	5.0	na
	2006	3.9	4.0	na	na	na	na	4.7	4.6	na
	2007	3.6	3.2	na	2.0	na	na	4.6	5.0	na
	2008	3.8	3.3	na	2.8	na	na	4.9	5.0	na
	2009	3.6	3.3	na	3.0	na	na	4.7	5.0	na
	2010	3.8	3.5	na	2.0	na	na	4.6	5.0	na
Starkey E	2005	4.0	na	na	2.0	na	na	1.0	na	na
	2006	4.6	na	na	2.0	na	na	1.0	na	na
	2007	4.0	na	na	1.0	na	na	1.0	na	na
	2008	4.5	na	na	1.2	na	na	1.0	na	na
	2009	4.2	na	na	1.0	na	na	na	na	na
	2010	3.9	na	na	1.0	na	na	na	na	na
Starkey N	2005	4.2	3.6	3.0	4.8	4.6	4.8	5.0	5.0	na
	2006	4.5	4.3	3.7	5.0	5.0	5.0	5.0	5.0	na
	2007	4.3	5.0	3.9	5.0	5.0	5.0	5.0	5.0	na
	2008	4.3	4.3	3.7	5.0	5.0	3.8	5.0	5.0	na
	2009	4.3	4.0	3.5	5.0	5.0	5.0	5.0	5.0	na
	2010	4.7	4.2	3.5	5.0	5.0	5.0	5.0	5.0	na
Starkey 108	2005	2.0	3.0	2.0	5.0	5.0	4.3	5.0	5.0	na
	2006	3.9	4.2	4.3	5.0	5.0	3.0	5.0	5.0	na
	2007	3.9	4.1	4.2	na	5.0	na	5.0	5.0	na
	2008	3.8	4.1	4.2	na	na	na	5.0	5.0	na
	2009	4.3	4.3	4.0	na	5.0	na	5.0	5.0	na
	2010	4.1	4.5	3.8	5.0	5.0	5.0	5.0	5.0	na

New River Marsh

The New River Marsh reference site is populated mostly with OBL and FACW plants. Vegetation in the center of the marsh is composed mostly of maidencane (*Panicum hemitomon*), with lesser amounts of pickerelweed (*Pontederia cordata*), Kissimmeegrass (*Paspalidium geminatum*), and manyflower marsh pennywort (*Hydrocotyle umbellata*). Blue maidencane (*Amphicarpum muhlenbergianum*) is common in the Outer Deep zone, with lesser amounts of manyflower marsh pennywort and maidencane. A few slash pines (*Pinus elliottii*) have encroached into the Outer Deep zone, but this is not unusual in northern Tampa Bay marshes (Michael Hancock, Southwest Florida Water Management District, unpub. data, 2009).

WAP scores for New River Marsh are indicative of a wetland that has water levels in the expected range for marshes in west-central Florida. The WAP scores for New River Marsh for groundcover ranged from 3 to 5 (table 4) and indicate typical groundcover, primarily OBL or FACW species; any signs of abnormal groundcover were limited to the Transition zone. The Deep zone is flooded when about 60 percent of the wetland is flooded (fig. 7D). The WAP scores ranged from 3 to 4 for shrubs and from 3 to 4 for trees (a WAP score of 3 at this marsh can reflect the minor encroachment of slash pine). Weighted-average scores for groundcover species remained between 4.0 and 5.0 (table 5). The scores for trees and shrubs (either na, not enough plant cover to make an evaluation, or 2.0) reflect either the characteristic absence of trees and shrubs in a marsh, or the limited presence of slash pine, which is an UPL species.

Q-1

Fallen or leaning cypress trees are an indication of hydrologic stress in Q-1 (Michael Hancock, Southwest Florida Water Management District, unpub. data, 2009). In 2006–2007, pond cypress was the dominant tree species, accounting for about 30 percent of the canopy cover. There were also small amounts of dahoon and swamp bay (*Persea palustris*) present. The subcanopy and shrub stratum was composed of cypress, but wax myrtle (*Myrica cerifera*) (FAC), swamp dogwood (*Cornus foemina*), and dahoon were present. Groundcover in the Deep zone was dominated by dogfennel (*Eupatorium capillifolium*) (FAC), swamp fern (*Blechnum serrulatum*), and fireweed (*Erechtites hieracifolia*) (FAC). Groundcover in the Transition zone was dominated by bushy bluestem (*Andropogon glomeratus*), blue maidencane, and dogfennel (Michael Hancock, Southwest Florida Water Management District, unpub. data, 2009).

The Deep and Outer Deep zones are flooded when 60 percent of Q-1 is flooded (fig. 8D). This extent of inundation did not occur in the pre-reduction period (fig. 8B), and it occurred in the post-reduction period only if rainfall was above average (during 2003–2004 as measured at the Saint Leo rainfall station). The WAP scores generally decreased at Q-1 during 2005–2008 (table 4). Scores for groundcover decreased from 3 to 2, scores for shrubs decreased from 3 to 2, and scores for tree species decreased from 5 to 3. The weighted-average scores for groundcover species decreased from 3.9 to 2.5 in the Deep zone, decreased from 3.2 to 2.1 in the Outer Deep zone, and did not show a trend in the Transition zone (table 5). Weighted-average scores for shrub species decreased from 4.4 to 3.3 in the Deep zone, decreased from 2.8 to 2.5 in the Outer Deep zone, and decreased from 3.5 to 2.1 in the Transition zone. Weighted-average scores remained about the same for tree species, and were 5.0 – 4.9 in the Deep zone, and 5.0 in the Outer Deep and Transition zones. Most of the Deep zone is flooded when 20 percent or more of the wetland is flooded (fig. 8D); but this extent of flooded area occurred only for brief periods after reductions in groundwater-withdrawal rates (fig. 8C).

W-17

An increasing cover of upland plants at W-17, including dogfennel (FAC), was observed as early as 1980 (EcoImpact, 1981), indicating persistently dry conditions. A detailed vegetative description of W-17 in 1987 indicated that the dominant canopy species were pond cypress, red maple (*Acer rubrum*), and swamp tupelo (*Nyssa sylvatica* var. *biflora*) (Michael Hancock, Southwest Florida Water Management District, unpub. data, 2009). Dominant shrubs were wax myrtle, fetterbush, red maple, and laurel oak (*Quercus laurifolia*). Dominant herbaceous species were break rush (*Rhynchospora* spp.), Virginia chainfern, sawgrass (*Cladium jamaicense*), arrowhead (*Sagittaria* spp.), and taperleaf waterhorehound.

The WAP data collected at W-17 during 2005–2008 indicated that there was little groundcover (less than 15 percent cover). Dogfennel and muscadine (*Vitis rotundifolia*) were dominant groundcover species. Cabbage palm (*Sabal palmetto*) (FAC), wax myrtle (FAC), and fetterbush were observed within the wetland. In the Deep zone of

Tree fall and evidence of subsidence at W-17.

the wetland, the dominant canopy species were cypress, red maple, and swamp tupelo, all OBL or FACW species. Slash pine, an UPL species, was observed in the Transition zone. Little change occurred in the WAP zonation scores for groundcover and shrubs during 2005–2008 (table 4), and scores for trees remained the same, indicating little change in hydrology during the period. Tree fall had been noted prior to 1987 and during 1994–1997 (Michael Hancock, Southwest Florida Water Management District, unpub. data, 2009).

Groundcover was generally low in coverage at W-17. Weighted-average scores decreased with time from 4.5 to 3.2 in the Deep zone, from 3.5 to 1.0 in the Outer Deep zone, and from 2.7 to 1.0 in the Transition zone (table 4). Weighted-average scores for shrubs were 3.0 in the Deep zone, and decreased from 3.3 to 2.5 in the Outer Deep zone and from 3.7 to 3.0 in the Transition zone (table 5). Weighted-average scores for tree species decreased from 4.9 to 4.5 in the Deep zone, 4.2 to 3.4 in the Outer Deep zone and 3.0 to 2.3 in the Transition zone. W-17 was dry for a smaller amount of time (30 percent less) after reductions in groundwater-withdrawal rates (fig. 9C). As much as 61–100 percent of the wetland was flooded for about 10 percent of the time during the post-reduction period, an extent of flooded area that includes the Deep and Outer Deep zones (fig. 9D). Although the extent and duration of the flooded area for W-17 appears to have increased after reductions in groundwater-withdrawal rates, the increase in flooded area was not reflected in increases in WAP scores or weighted-average scores.

W-33

W-33 is populated with OBL tree species, including cypress and swamp tupelo, and the understory consists of OBL and FACW species including dahoon, red maple, fetterbush, and buttonbush (Michael Hancock, Southwest Florida Water Management District, unpub. data, 2009; Reynolds, Smith, and Hills, Inc., 2001). Groundcover species included lesser creeping rush, arrowhead, waterhyssop (*Bacopa* spp.), beaksedge, bladderwort (*Utricularia* spp.), and Virginia chainfern. Vegetation assessments in 2007 indicated that dominant groundcover species included Virginia chainfern, caric sedge (*Carex* spp.), narrowfruit horned beaksedge (*Rhynchospora inundata*), and bushy bluestem (*Andropogon glomeratus)*. Saw palmetto (*Serenoa repens*) was the dominant shrub species in the Transition zone.

WAP scores for W-33 for groundcover varied from 3 to 4 during 2005–2008 (table 4). Scores for shrubs (5) and trees (5) were high and unchanged during 2005–2008. Weighted-average scores for groundcover increased slightly during the period. Scores ranged from 4.1 to 4.3 in the Deep zone, 3.7 to 4.0 in the Outer Deep zone and 3.4 to 3.7 in the Transition zone. Scores for shrubs remained the same at 5.0 in the Deep and Outer Deep zones, and increased in the Transition zone from 2.0 to 3.5 (table 5). The Deep and Outer Deep zones are flooded when 40 percent or more of the wetland is flooded (fig. 10D), an extent of the flooded area that was reached

41 percent of the time during the pre-reduction period and 49 percent of the time during the post-reduction period. The large extent and long duration of flooded area are reflected in the high weighted-average scores for trees (4.9 – 5.0) in the Deep, Outer Deep, and Transition zones.

W-41

W-41 has a canopy dominated by cypress trees. Other abundant trees and shrubs are red maple, laurel oak, dahoon, buttonbush, southern magnolia (*Magnolia grandiflora*), and wax myrtle (Southwest Florida Water Management District, 2009). Slash pine (UPL), American elm (*Ulmus americanus*) (FACW) and live oak (*Quercus virginiana*) (UPL) also were observed. Groundcover includes taperleaf waterhorehound, false daisy (*Eclipta prostrata*) (FACW), Long's sedge (*Carex longii*) (FACW), dogfennel (FAC), *Panicum* spp., and American beautyberry (*Callicarpa americana*) (UPL). Shrub species include saw palmetto, fetterbush, American beautyberry, wax myrtle, and sweet gum (*Liquidambar styraciflua)* (Michael Hancock, Southwest Florida Water Management District, unpub. data, 2009).

The WAP scores for W-41 for groundcover, shrubs, and trees were generally low (2) during 2005–2008 with a small but temporary increase from 2 to 3 for groundcover and shrubs during 2006 (table 4). The Deep zone is not completely flooded until about 50 percent of the wetland is flooded (fig. 11D) and the flooded area rarely reached that extent even after reductions in groundwater-withdrawal rates (fig. 11C). Weighted-average scores for groundcover in the Deep zone decreased from 3.8 to 1.5 during 2006–2008 (table 5). The amount of groundcover was generally low in all zones and weighted-average scores were 2.4 to 2.3 in the Outer Deep zone and 2.2 to 2.8 in the Transition zone during 2006–2007. Shrub scores declined from 3.3 to 2.5 in the Deep zone, and were low in the Outer Deep zone (1.0), and the Transition zone (1.3). Tree scores declined slightly from 4.4 to 4.3 in the Deep zone, and remained at 3.0 in the Outer Deep and Transition zones. A small amount of groundcover was present in the Deep zone in 2008, but plant cover was not sufficient to make an evaluation. Although up to 20 percent of the wetland was flooded for 15 percent of the time after reductions in groundwater-withdrawal rates, W-41 remained dry for 75 percent of the time.

W-56

The dominant tree species in W-56 are pond cypress and swamp tupelo. Shrubs include saw palmetto, peelbark St. John's-wort (*Hypericum fasciculatum*), swamp bay, wax myrtle, buttonbush, and sabal palm. Vegetation in the inner part of the wetland includes lesser creeping rush, *Lycopus* sp., and Virginia buttonweed (*Diodia virginiana*). The outer part of the wetland includes maidencane, branched hedge-hyssop (*Gratiola ramosa),* tenangle pipewort (*Eriocaulon decangulare)*, Virginia buttonweed and rosy camphorweed (*Pluchea baccharis)* (Michael Hancock, Southwest Florida Water Management District, unpub. data, 2009).

The WAP scores for W-56 during 2005–2008 varied from 3 to 4 for groundcover, increased from 4 to 5 for shrubs, and were unchanged at 4 for trees (table 4). Weighted-average scores for groundcover in the Deep zone were 4.0 to 4.5 (table 5), and the most abundant species were OBL or FACW species. The Deep zone is flooded in W-56 when about 40 percent of the wetland is flooded (fig. 12*D*). About 41–100 percent of the wetland was flooded 16 percent of the time before reductions in groundwater-withdrawal rates and about 14 percent of the time after reductions. Therefore, the extent and duration of the flooded area can support OBL vegetation in the Deep zone. Groundcover weighted averages declined slightly from 4.5 to 4.2 in the Outer Deep zone during the period after reductions (table 5). Common shrubs and trees were primarily OBL species, and weighted-average scores for shrubs and trees were 4.9 to 5.0 in the Deep and Outer Deep zones (table 5). Plant coverages in the Transition zone were not sufficient to make an evaluation for shrubs and trees. Patterns of inundation before and after reductions in groundwater-withdrawal rates at W-56 indicate that the wetland was dry about 25 percent less time and up to 20 percent of the wetland was flooded four times longer during the post-reduction period (fig. 12*C*).

Starkey D

Vegetation sampling has occurred at Starkey D since 1975 and dry conditions were indicated by the invasion of slash pines, an UPL species, in the early 1980s. This UPL species has reached canopy to subcanopy heights in recent years (Michael Hancock, Southwest Florida Water Management District, unpub. data, 2009). The small extent and brief duration of flooded area in Starkey D have not been sufficient to halt continued slash pine establishment and growth. The understory is composed of chainfern, waterhorehound, dogfennel, and bluestem (*Andropogon* spp.). Increasing abundance of chainfern in recent years is attributed to dry conditions in the wetland and the occasional occurrence of fire (Michael Hancock, Southwest Florida Water Management District, unpub. data, 2009). Considerable wax myrtle and young common persimmon (*Diospyros. virginiana*) were observed on the ground in the Deep zone in 2005. These two FAC species are not typically in the Deep zone of healthy cypress wetlands. The departure from normal shrub and young tree zonation is attributed to persistent low wetland water levels.

The WAP scores during 2005–2010 for groundcover in Starkey D increased from 2 to 3, but WAP scores for shrubs (2) and trees (2) were consistently low during the period (table 4). Weighted-average scores for groundcover decreased slightly from 4.0 to 3.8 in the Deep zone and increased from 1.0 to 3.5 in the Outer Deep zone (table 3).

The most abundant groundcover species were Virginia chainfern (FACW) and warty sedge (FACW). Cabbage palm (FAC) and common persimmon (FAC) were also present. The Deep zone at Starkey D is flooded when about 60 percent of the wetland is flooded (fig. 13*D*). Therefore, the Deep zone was rarely flooded, and when inundation occurred, it was for a very brief duration during either the pre- or post-reduction periods (fig. 13*C*). Weighted-average scores for shrubs ranged from 2.0 to 3.0 in the Deep zone (table 5). FAC species such as wax myrtle and cabbage palm in the Deep zone contributed to the lower scores. The abundance of pond cypress in the Deep and Outer Deep zones kept weighted-average scores for trees high, from 4.6 to 5.0, but slash pine (FAC) was also present in the Deep and Outer Deep zones. Plant cover was not sufficient in the Transition zone to allow for an evaluation.

Starkey E

Dry conditions at Starkey E have allowed blue maidencane (FACW) to spread downslope from the edge of the marsh, and dogfennel (FAC), *Andropogon* spp., and redroot (FAC) (*Lachnanthes caroliana*) have spread across the marsh center in some years (Southwest Florida Water Management District, 2009). Invasive species in the marsh center die during wet years and the central wet area becomes open water. As a result of instability in marsh vegetation and plant zonation, the wetland appears very different from natural wetlands. Instability in marsh vegetation is most likely due to fluctuating wetland water levels from nearby groundwater pumping. Deep and widespread soil fissuring has been observed and overall subsidence of the marsh center has occurred, resulting in the unusual depth of this wetland (> 11 ft). A conspicuous soil slump not far from the staff gage has occurred, most likely caused by persistent low water levels (Michael Hancock, Southwest Florida Water Management District, unpub. data, 2009).

The WAP scores at Starkey E for groundcover, shrubs, and trees were consistently low during 2005–2010 (table 4). Weighted-average scores for groundcover ranged from 4.0 to 4.6 in the Deep zone (table 5), where OBL species such as falsefennel (*Eupatorium leptophyllum*) and maidencane, and FACW species including blue maidencane and *Rhynchospora* sp. were present. Scores for shrubs generally declined from 2.0 to 1.0 during the 6-year period and scores for tree species were low (1.0) in the Deep zone, symptomatic of the presence of UPL species including sand pine, and FAC species including live oak, which would not be expected in a marsh. The Deep zone is not completely flooded until about 80 percent of the wetland is flooded (fig. 14*D*). During the post-reduction period, less than 20 percent of the wetland was flooded 80 percent of the time (fig. 14*C*), and the Outer Deep and Transition zones were not flooded. Plant coverage was not sufficient to allow for WAP evaluation in those zones.

Starkey N

Vegetation in Starkey N was monitored since 1980. Monitoring results indicate relatively little vegetation change in the interior of the wetland, but vegetation changes in the outer part of the wetland near the cypress fringe are more evident. Blue maidencane has become more abundant than in earlier years; blue maidencane in the northern Tampa Bay region has become more common and encroaches into cypress and marsh wetlands when water levels are lower than average (Michael Hancock, Southwest Florida Water Management District, unpub. data, 2009).

At Starkey N the stability in the vegetation community as described in the WAP scores and weighted average scores is likely due to the increased extent and duration of the flooded area during the post-reduction period, when the wetland was flooded throughout 81–100 percent of its total area for 53 percent of the time (fig. 15C). The WAP scores for groundcover remained at 4, with the exception of 2007 when the score was 3. Scores for shrubs (5) and trees (5) were high and remained unchanged during 2005–2010 (table 4). Weighted-average scores for groundcover increased slightly from 4.2 to 4.7 in the Deep zone, increased from 3.6 to 4.2 in the Outer Deep zone, and increased from 3.0 to 3.5 in the Transition zone (table 5). Groundcover plant species identified in the Deep zone were OBL or FACW species. Scores for shrub species increased slightly from 4.6 or 4.8 to 5.0 in all zones. The presence of wax myrtle lowered one score in the Transition zone to 3.8, but this FAC species is present in the Transition zone of many wetlands in the northern Tampa Bay region. Tree species in the Deep and Outer Deep zones were OBL and the weighted-average scores were unchanged at 5.0 during 2005–2010. The Deep zone is flooded when about 60 percent of the total wetland area is flooded (fig. 15D), and this extent of the flooded area occurred 64 percent of the time during the post-reduction period.

Wetland vegetation near the staff gage and wetland well at Starkey N.

Starkey 108

Vegetation monitoring in Starkey 108 indicated that obligate wetland plants, including sawgrass, bulltongue arrowhead (*Sagittaria lancifolia*), pickerelweed, and lizard's tail (*Saururus cernuus*) were common in the wetland (Michael Hancock, Southwest Florida Water Management District, unpub. data, 2009). FAC species including dogfennel and wax myrtle were observed during drier periods and became increasingly abundant in cypress-dominated areas of the wetland (Michael Hancock, Southwest Florida Water Management District, unpub. data, 2009).

The WAP scores for groundcover in Starkey 108 during the post-reduction period varied from 3 to 4, whereas shrub scores (5) and tree scores (5) were unchanged (table 4). Weighted-average scores for groundcover increased in all zones, from 2.0 to 4.1 in the Deep zone, from 3.0 to 4.5 in the Outer Deep zone, and from 2.0 to 3.8 in the Transition zone (table 5). Warty sedge (FACW) and Virginia chainfern (FACW) were abundant groundcover species in the Deep and Outer Deep zones. The Deep zone is flooded in Starkey 108 when about 20 percent of the wetland is flooded (fig. 16D), and during the post-reduction period 21 percent or more of the wetland was flooded for 46 percent of the time (fig. 16C). Weighted-average scores for shrubs were high (5.0) in the Deep and Outer Deep zones, and varied from 3.0 to 5.0 in the Transition zone, where plant coverage was often too low to make an evaluation. Weighted-average scores were also high for trees (5) in the Deep and Outer Deep zones, due to the abundance of pond cypress (OBL) and swamp tupelo (OBL).

Plant Zonation Summary

WAP scores and weighted-average scores were consistently high at the reference wetlands Green Swamp Cypress and New River Marsh during 2005–2008. These scores indicate the prevalence and persistence of OBL and FACW plants that typically are present in the flooded areas of unimpaired marsh and cypress wetlands in the northern Tampa Bay region. The extent and duration of the flooded area at the reference wetlands also reflect the absence of impairment at the reference sites.

The WAP scores and weighted-average scores for four of the nine study wetlands in well fields (W-33, W-56, Starkey N, and Starkey 108) were higher overall compared to the other five well-field wetlands, and they remained high or increased during the post-reduction period. Scores for trees were more consistent than scores for shrubs and groundcover. These four wetlands had increases in the extent and duration of the flooded area, and the potentiometric surface of the Upper Floridan aquifer in the vicinity of these wetlands also increased when the pre- and post-reduction periods were compared.

The WAP scores at the other five study wetlands (Q-1, W-17, W-41, Starkey D, Starkey E) were relatively low for the duration of the study period and weighted-average scores either remained low or generally declined over time, although there were exceptions. The WAP scores and weighted-average scores for groundcover and shrubs were low and generally declined at Q-1, Starkey D, and W-41, whereas scores for trees did not change. With the exception of W-17 and Q-1, none of these five wetlands demonstrated an increase in the duration or extent of the flooded area following reductions in groundwater-withdrawal rates. W-17 and Q-1 had small increases in the extent of the flooded area, but these wetlands remained dry for 65 and 82 percent of the time, respectively.

The reduced extent and duration of flooded area in well-field wetlands has affected the aquatic vegetation communities in those wetlands by reducing the abundance and altering the distribution patterns of OBL and FACW plant species, and by increasing the abundance of FAC and UPL species within the wetland perimeter. Changes in the distribution of wetland plants from one year to the next are described in the annual WAP. However, the period of time for which WAP scores were available for this study was relatively short (4–6 years), and may not have been sufficient to reveal trends in plant zonation. Hydrologic changes precede and ultimately lead to changes in wetland vegetation, but the time-averaged duration of the hydrologic changes that result in vegetation changes are not yet well known.

Summary

Hundreds of wetlands in west-central Florida are located in well fields where groundwater withdrawals from the Upper Floridan aquifer occur. Groundwater withdrawals from the Upper Floridan aquifer have lowered the potentiometric surface of the aquifer and induced downward leakage from the overlying water table in the surficial aquifer. Water-level declines in the underlying surficial aquifer also have induced downward leakage from wetlands in well fields, which has reduced wetland hydroperiod. The induced leakage has altered the hydrology of many isolated wetlands that are located in well fields. Changes in hydrologic conditions can alter vegetation communities in wetlands, and these vegetation changes can diminish available habitat and render wetlands less suitable for wildlife.

In response to concerns about declining water levels of wetlands in well fields, reductions in well-field groundwater-withdrawal rates were initiated by the regional utility Tampa Bay Water. Reductions in groundwater-withdrawal rates from Cypress Creek well field and Cross Bar Ranch well field were initiated in September 2002, whereas reductions from Starkey well field were initiated in 2007. A comparison of pre- and post-reduction periods indicates that the median elevation of the potentiometric surface of the Upper Floridan aquifer has risen in parts of the Cross Bar Ranch, Cypress Creek, and Starkey well fields, as a direct result of these reductions. Following the reductions in groundwater-withdrawal rates, and the resulting increase in the median elevation of the potentiometric surface of the Upper Floridan aquifer,

downward leakage has been reduced, and water levels in some wetlands have recovered, although others have not. This study was undertaken to determine the extent and duration of the flooded area in isolated wetlands in well fields before and after reductions in groundwater-withdrawal rates and the relation between wetland flooded area and plant zonation.

The extent and duration of the flooded area was quantified at two reference wetlands and nine wetlands in well fields during the pre- and post-reduction periods. Total rainfall amounts were similar (differed by 1 percent or less) during the respective pre- and post-reduction periods, which minimized the effect that rainfall variability had on the analysis of all wetlands. Inundation patterns at the Green Swamp Cypress reference wetland were similar during the pre- and post-reduction periods applied to the wetlands in the Cypress Creek and Cross Bar Ranch well fields, indicating that short-term (year-to-year) variability in rainfall did not affect the longer-term flooded area frequencies of this unimpacted wetland. Inundation patterns were somewhat similar at the New River Marsh reference wetland during the pre- and post-reduction periods, but the period of record at this site did not overlap the entire pre-reduction period.

Only one well-field wetland (W-33) experienced the extent and duration of inundation similar to that observed at the reference wetlands either before or after reductions in groundwater-withdrawal rates. Water levels in W-33 reached normal pool both before and after reductions in groundwater-withdrawal rates, and increments of the total wetland area were flooded for similar periods of time before and after reductions. The median elevation of the potentiometric surface of the Upper Floridan aquifer was about 3 ft higher beneath this wetland during the post-reduction period when the pre- and post-reduction periods are compared.

Four study wetlands in Cypress Creek well field and Cross Bar Ranch well field were mostly dry before reductions in groundwater-withdrawal rates. Two of those four wetlands (W-56 and W-17) had increases in the extent and duration of the flooded area after reductions in groundwater-withdrawal rates, and both were dry 25–30 percent less time. The median elevation of the potentiometric surface of the Upper Floridan aquifer was about 4–7 ft higher beneath these two wetlands during the post-reduction period, when the pre-and post-reduction periods are compared, and this increase was the primary cause of increases in wetland flooded area. The other two wetlands (W-41 and Q-1) remained mostly dry even after reductions in groundwater-withdrawal rates. Although W-41 was dry for less time in the post-reduction period, most of the increased inundation was confined to less than 20 percent of the total wetland area. The median elevation of the Upper Floridan aquifer increased beneath W-41 by about 5 ft when the pre- and post-reduction periods are compared, although it remained about 9 ft below the wetland bottom. Q-1 was dry for 12 percent less time in the post-reduction period, when the pre-and post-reduction periods were compared. The median elevation of the Upper Floridan aquifer increased beneath Q-1 about 2 ft after reductions in groundwater-withdrawal rates. Even though the median elevation of the potentiometric surface increased, it remained about 6 ft below the wetland bottom. Additional factors, such as high permeability of sediments beneath the wetlands, subsidence, or sinkholes, could have contributed to the lack of recovery at W-41 and Q-1.

Two of the four study wetlands in the Starkey well field (Starkey N and Starkey 108) had flooded areas that increased in extent and duration during the post-reduction period compared to the pre-reduction period. Starkey N and Starkey 108 were dry for 45 and 38 percent less time, respectively, and the median elevation of the potentiometric surface of the Upper Floridan aquifer increased beneath these wetlands by about 4 ft after reductions in groundwater-withdrawal rates.

The other two wetlands in Starkey well field (Starkey D and Starkey E) did not experience an increase in the duration or extent of the flooded area after reductions in groundwater-withdrawal rates. Inundation patterns were either unchanged or the extent of the flooded area decreased slightly during the post-reduction period when the pre-and post-reduction periods were compared. The median elevation of the potentiometric surface of the Upper Floridan aquifer did not increase beneath either of these wetlands after reductions in groundwater-withdrawal rates, and therefore downward leakage from these wetlands was not diminished.

Plant zonation at the two reference wetlands and the nine wetlands in well fields was described using data collected by the Southwest Florida Water Management District and Tampa Bay Water in their Wetland Assessment Procedure (WAP). A scoring system was used to describe the distribution of trees, woody shrubs, and groundcover in zones at three depths along a transect line through each wetland. The locations of the three zones were identified on contoured wetland bathymetry maps and were discussed in relation to increments of the total wetland area that flooded for different periods of time during the study. Higher scores are characteristic of wetlands with a greater extent and duration of flooded area.

WAP scores and weighted-average scores for wetland vegetation were generally consistent with the results of the flooded-area analysis for the 3- or 4-year periods following reductions in groundwater-withdrawal rates when data were available to make the comparison. The WAP scores and weighted-average scores were higher overall and did not decline at four of the study wetlands in well fields

(W-33, W-56, Starkey N, and Starkey 108) during the years following reductions in groundwater-withdrawal rates. These four wetlands also demonstrated increases in the extent and duration of the flooded area following reductions. Scores for trees were more consistent than scores for shrubs and groundcover at these sites. WAP scores remained relatively low or generally declined at the other five wetlands in well fields (Q-1, W-17, W-41, Starkey D, and Starkey E) during the years following reductions in groundwater-withdrawal rates, and weighted-average scores either declined over time or remained low. These five wetlands either did not have an increase in the duration or extent of the flooded area, or if there was an increase, it was small.

WAP scores and weighted-average scores were not unequivocal indicators of change in the duration or extent of the flooded area in well-field wetlands in this study. For example, at some wetlands groundcover and shrub scores were generally lower or declined with time more than scores for trees. Also, although flooded area did increase modestly at W-17, the WAP and weighted-average scores remained low or decreased. In addition, the period of time for which WAP scores were available was relatively short (3–4 years). Hydrologic changes precede and ultimately lead to changes in wetland vegetation; however, the time-averaged duration of the hydrologic changes that result in vegetation changes are not well known and can range from one season to several years.

Wetland flooded-area estimates can provide a comprehensive understanding of wetland hydrology over time and for wetlands of different sizes. Although hydrograph data for a particular year indicate water levels at the staff gage, flooded-area estimates during a period of several years can indicate the extent of the wetland area that is routinely flooded and is consequently available to provide functional habitat for wetland plants. Many wetland plants, including trees and shrubs, respond to prevailing patterns in the extent and duration of the flooded area that persist for more than one season or one year, and wetland plant distribution may be more predictably influenced by those patterns than by wetland water levels measured at the staff gage. WAP data can provide another line of evidence to describe the relations between groundwater levels, the extent and duration of wetland flooded area, and the vegetation that creates functional wetland habitat.

References Cited

Atkinson, R.B., Perry, J.E., Smith, E.P., Cairns Jr., John, 1993, Use of created wetland delineation and weighted averages as a component of assessment: Wetlands, v. 13, p. 185–193.

Balcombe, C.K., Anderson, A.T., Fortney, R.H., Rentch, J.S., Grafton, W.N., and Kordek, W.S., 2005, A comparison of plant communities in mitigation and reference wetlands in the mid-Appalachians: Wetlands, v. 25, no. 1, p. 130–142.

Berryman & Henigar, Inc., 1995, Phase I: Evaluation of groundwater augmentation of wetland and aquatic habitats: Clearwater, Fla., Consultant's report prepared for West Coast Regional Water Supply Authority, 45 p.

Berryman & Henigar, Inc., 2000, Phase II: Evaluation of groundwater augmentation of wetland and aquatic habitats: Clearwater, Fla., Consultant's report prepared for West Coast Regional Water Supply Authority, 95 p.

Berryman & Henigar, Inc., 2001, J.B. Starkey Well Field and North Pasco Regional Well Field ecological/hydrological monitoring program, water year 2000 annual monitoring report: Clearwater, Fla., Consultant's report prepared for Tampa Bay Water, variously paged.

Biological Research Associates, Inc., 1996, Use of lasting indicators of historic inundation patterns in isolated wetlands as reference elevations to determine areal extent and intensity of reduced water levels near areas of groundwater withdrawals: Clearwater, Fla., Consultant's report prepared for Tampa Bay Water, 10 p.

Biological Research Associates, Inc., 2001, Hydrological and ecological environmental assessment report for the Cross Bar Ranch Wellfield, Water Year 2000: Clearwater, Fla., Consultant's report prepared for Tampa Bay Water, variously paged.

Biological Research Associates, Inc., and Berryman & Henigar, Inc., 2006, Field identification guide to plants used in the Wetland Assessment Procedure (WAP), Brooksville, Fla., Consultants report prepared for the Southwest Florida Water Management District, 59 p.

Carr, D.W., Leeper, D.A., and Rochow, T.F., 2006, Comparison of six biologic indicators of hydrology and the landward extent of hydric soils in west-central Florida, USA cypress domes: Wetlands, no. 26, p. 1012–1019.

Dwire, K.A., Kauffman, J.B., Baham, J.E., 2006, Plant species distribution in relation to water-table depth and soil redox potential in montane riparian meadows: Wetlands, v. 26, no. 1, p. 131–146.

EcoImpact, 1981, Ecological monitoring of the Cypress Creek Wellfield and vicinity—August 1979 through September 1981: Consultant's report prepared for the West Coast Regional Water Supply Authority.

Haag, K.H. and Lee, T.M., 2006, Flooding frequency alters vegetation in isolated wetlands: U.S. Geological Survey Fact Sheet 2006–3117, 4 p.

Haag, K.H., and Lee, T.M., 2010, Hydrology and ecology of freshwater wetlands in central Florida —A primer: U.S. Geological Survey Circular 1342, 138 p.

Haag, K.H., Lee, T.M., and Herndon, D.C., 2005, Bathymetry and vegetation in isolated marsh and cypress wetlands in the Northern Tampa Bay area: U.S. Geological Survey Scientific Investigations Report 2005–5109, 49 p.

Hancock, M.C., 1999, Establishment of recovery levels in the Northern Tampa Bay area: Brooksville, Fla., Southwest Florida Water Management District, 229 p.

Hancock, M.C., Rochow, T.F., and Hood, Jason, 2005, Test results of a proposed revision to the Wetland Assessment Procedure (WAP), October 2004 and development of the final wetland assessment methodology adopted in April 2005: Brooksville, Fla., Southwest Florida Water Management District report, 147 p.

Hull, H.C., Post, J.M. Lopez, Manny, and Perry, R.G., 1989, Analysis of water-level indicators in wetlands: Implications for the design of surface water management systems, *in* Wetlands: Concerns and successes: Proceedings of the American Water Resources Association, Tampa, Fla., p. 195–204.

Hutchinson, M.F., and Gessler, P.E., 1994, Splines—More than just a smooth interpolator: Geoderma, v. 62, p. 45–67.

Jones Edmunds & Associates, Inc., 2010, Wetland classification and basin character study—Wetland hydrologic analysis: Brooksville, Fla., Consultant's report prepared for the Southwest Florida Water Management District, 47 p.

Kennedy, T.A., 2010, Levels at gaging stations: U.S. Geological Survey Techniques of Water-Resources Investigations 3–A19, 60 p.

Lane, C.R., and D'Amico, Ellen, 2010, Calculating the ecosystem service of water storage in isolated wetlands using LIDAR in north central Florida: Wetlands, 30, p. 967–977.

Lee, T.M., and Haag, K.H., 2006, Strength in numbers: describing the flooded area of isolated wetlands: U.S. Geological Survey Fact Sheet 2006–3118, 4 p.

Lee, T.M., Haag, K.H., Metz, P.A., and Sacks, L.A., 2009, The comparative hydrology, water quality, and ecology of selected natural and augmented freshwater wetlands in west-central Florida: U.S. Geological Survey Professional Paper 1758, 152 p.

Marella, R.L., 2009, Water withdrawals, use, and trends in Florida, 2005: U.S. Geological Survey Scientific Investigations Report 2009–5125, 49 p.

Metz, P.A., 2011, Factors that influence the hydrologic recovery of wetlands in the northern Tampa Bay area: U.S. Geological Survey Scientific Investigations Report 2011–5127, 58 p.

Metz, P.A., and Sacks, L.A., 2002, Comparison of the hydrogeology and water quality of a ground-water augmented lake with two non-augmented lakes in northwest Hillsborough County, Florida: U.S. Geological Survey Water-Resources Investigations Report 02–4032, 74 p.

Metz, P.A., Delzer, G.C., Berndt, M.P., Crandall, C.A., and Toccalino, P.L., 2007, Anthropogenic organic compounds in ground water and finished water of community water systems in the Northern Tampa Bay area, Florida, 2002–04: U.S. Geological Survey Scientific Investigations Report 5267, 48 p.

National Oceanic and Atmospheric Administration, 2010, Temperature, precipitation, drought data for Florida: National Oceanic and Atmospheric Administration Climate Division, accessed February 8, 2010, at *http://www1.ncdc. noaa.gov/pub/data/cirs/drd964x.pcp.txt.*

Reed, P.B., Jr., 1988, National list of plant species that occur in wetlands: Southeast (Region 2): Fort Collins, Colo., U.S. Fish and Wildlife Service Biological Report 88 (26.2), 140 p.

Reynolds, Smith, and Hills, Inc., 2001, Final annual comprehensive report: Ecological and hydrological monitoring of the Cypress Creek Wellfield and vicinity, Pasco County, Florida: Tampa, Consultant's report prepared for Tampa Bay Water, variously paged.

Rochow, T.F., 1998, The effects of water table level changes on fresh-water marsh and cypress wetlands: Brooksville, Fla., Southwest Florida Water Management District Environmental Section Technical Report 1998–1, 64 p.

Rochow, T.F., and Lopez, Manny, 1984, Hydrobiological monitoring of cypress domes in the Green Swamp area of Lake and Sumter Counties, Florida, 1979–1982: Brooksville, Fla., Southwest Florida Water Management District Environmental Section Technical Report 1984–1, 79 p.

Schultz, R.W., Hancock, M.C., Hood, Jason, Carr, D.W., and Rochow, T.F., 2004, Use of biologic indicators for the establishment of historic normal pool: Brooksville, Fla., Southwest Florida Water Management District, 13 p.

Southwest Florida Water Management District and Tampa Bay Water, 2005, Wetland Assessment Procedure (WAP) instruction manual for isolated wetlands, March 2005: Brooksville, Southwest Florida Water Management District report.

Tampa Bay Water, 2000, Environmental Management Plan for the Tampa Bay Water Central System well fields: Clearwater, Florida, 58 p.

Tampa Bay Water, 2004, Optimized regional operations plan annual report July 2004: Clearwater, Florida, Report prepared for Southwest Florida Water Management District, 36 p.

Tampa Bay Water, 2008, Optimized regional operations plan WY 2007: Clearwater, Florida, Report prepared for the Southwest Florida Water Management District, variously paged.

Tampa Bay Water, 2010, Optimized regional operations plan WY 2009: Clearwater, Florida, Report prepared for Southwest Florida Water Management District, 20 p.

Tampa Bay Water, 2011, Groundwater cutbacks: Accessed October 25, 2011, at *http://www.tampabaywater.org/ supplies/.*

Tihansky, A.B., 1999, Sinkholes in west-central Florida, *in* Galloway, Devin, Jones, D.R., Ingebritsen, S.E., eds., Land subsidence in the United States: U.S. Geological Survey Circular 1182, p. 121–140.

Torres, A.E., Haag, K.H., Lee, T.M., and Metz, P.A., 2011, USGS research on Florida's isolated freshwater wetlands: U.S. Geological Survey Fact Sheet 2011–3094, 4 p.

Toth, L.A., 2005, Plant community structure and temporal variability in a channelized subtropical floodplain: Southeastern Naturalist, v. 4, no. 3, p. 393–408.

U.S. Environmental Protection Agency, 2002, Methods for evaluating wetland condition–#10: Using vegetation to assess environmental conditions in wetlands: Washington, D.C., EPA–822–R–02–020, 38 p.

Wentworth, T.R., Johnson, G.P., and Kologiski, R.L., 1988, Designation of wetland by weighted averages of vegetation data: A preliminary evaluation: Water Resources Bulletin, v. 24, no. 2, p. 389–396.

White, W.A., 1970, The geomorphology of the Florida peninsula: Tallahassee, Fla., Florida Bureau of Geology Bulletin 5, 164 p.

Wilcox, Chris, and Huertos, M.L., 2005, A simple rapid method for mapping bathymetry of small wetland basins: Journal of Hydrology, v. 301, p. 29–36.

Wunderlin, R.P., and Hansen, B.F., 2010, Atlas of Florida vascular plants, accessed January 8, 2010, at *http://www. florida.plantatlas.usf.edu/about.aspx.*

Appendixes 1–12

Appendix 1. List of plants identified in study wetlands, including index values, FDEP status, and WAP status.

[FDEP, Florida Department of Environmental Protection; WAP, Wetland Assessment Procedure; FACW, facultative wetland species; OD, outer deep zone; FAC, facultative species; T, transition zone; UPL, upland species; na, not available; OBL, obligate wetland species; AD, adaptive species; U, upland species; D, deep zone]

Genus	Species	Abbreviation	Index value	FDEP status	WAP status	Common name
Acer	*rubrum*	*A. rubrum*	4	FACW	OD	Red maple
Amphicarpum	*muhlenbergianum*	*A. muhlenbergianum*	4	FACW	OD	Blue maidencane
Andropogon	*glomeratus*	*A. glomeratus*	3	FACW	T	Bushy bluestem
Andropogon	*virginicus*	*A. virginicus*	2	FAC	AD	Broomsedge bluestem
Aristida	*stricta beyrichiana*	*A. stricta*	3	FAC	na	Wiregrass
Axonopus	sp.	*Axonopus* sp.	2	FAC	AD	Carpetgrass
Bacopa	sp.	*Bacopa* sp.	5	OBL	OD	Waterhyssop
Blechnum	*serrulatum*	*B. serrulatum*	4	FACW	na	Swamp fern
Callicarpa	*americana*	*C. americana*	1	UPL	U	American beautyberry
Campsis	*radicans*	*C. radicans*	2	FAC	T	Trumpet creeper
Carex	*verrucosa*	*C. verrucosa*	4	FACW	na	Warty sedge
Carex	*longii*	*C. longii*	3	FACW	T	Long's sedge
Cephalanthus	*occidentalis*	*C. occidentalis*	5	OBL	D	Buttonbush
Cladium	*jamaicense*	*C. jamaicense*	5	OBL	na	Jamaica swamp sawgrass
Coelorachis	*rugosa*	*C. rugosa*	4	FACW	na	Wrinkled jointailgrass
Commelina	*diffusa*	*C. diffusa*	3	FACW	T	Common dayflower
Conyza	*canadensis*	*C. canadensis*	2	na	AD	Canadian horseweed
Cornus	*foemina*	*C. foemina*	4	FACW	OD	Swamp dogwood
Dichanthelium	*commutatum*	*D. commutatum*	3	FAC	na	Variable witchgrass
Diodia	*virginiana*	*D. virginiana*	4	FACW	OD	Virginia buttonweed
Diospyros	*virginiana*	*D. virginiana*	2	FAC	AD	Common persimmon
Drosera	sp.	*Drosera* sp.	4	FACW	na	Sundew
Drymaria	*cordata*	*D. cordata*	2	FAC	AD	West Indian chickweed
Eclipta	*prostrata*	*E. prostrata*	3	FACW	T	False daisy
Erechtites	*hieracifolia*	*E. hieracifolia*	2	FAC	AD	Fireweed
Eriocaulon	*decangulare*	*E. decangulare*	5	OBL	na	Tenangle pipewort
Eupatorium	*capillifolium*	*E. capillifolium*	2	FAC	AD	Dogfennel
Eupatorium	*leptophyllum*	*E. leptophyllum*	5	OBL	OD	Falsefennel
Galactia	*Elliottii*	*G. elliottii*	1	na	U	Elliott's milkpea
Gratiola	*ramosa*	*G. ramosa*	3	FACW	T	Branched hedgehyssop
Hydrocotyle	*umbellata*	*H. umbellata*	4	FACW	OD	Manyflower marshpennywort
Hypericum	*fasciculatum*	*H. fasciculatum*	5	OBL	OD	Peelbark St.John's-wort
Ilex	*cassine*	*I. cassine*	5	OBL	OD	Dahoon
Juncus	*repens*	*J. repens*	5	OBL	na	Lesser creeping rush
Lachnanthes	*caroliana*	*L. caroliana*	3	FAC	na	Carolina redroot
Liquidambar	*styraciflua*	*L. styraciflua*	3	FACW	T	Sweetgum
Ludwigia	*peruviana*	*L. peruviana*	5	OBL	OD	Peruvian primrosewillow
Lycopus	*rubellus*	*L. rubellus*	5	OBL	OD	Taperleaf waterhorehound
Lyonia	*lucida*	*L. lucida*	3	FACW	T	Fetterbush
Magnolia	*virginiana*	*M. virginiana*	5	OBL	OD	Sweetbay
Magnolia	*grandiflora*	*M. grandiflora*	3	FAC	na	Southern magnolia
Mikania	*scandens*	*M. scandens*	3	FACW	T	Climbing hempvine
Myrica	*cerifera*	*M. cerifera*	2	FAC	AD	Wax myrtle

Appendix 1. List of plants identified in study wetlands, including index values, FDEP status, and WAP status—Continued.

[FDEP, Florida Department of Environmental Protection; WAP, Wetland Assessment Procedure; FACW, facultative wetland species; OD, outer deep zone; FAC, facultative species; T, transition zone; UPL, upland species; na, not available; OBL, obligate wetland species; AD, adaptive species; U, upland species; D, deep zone]

Genus	Species	Abbreviation	Index value	FDEP status	WAP status	Common name
Nyssa	*sylvatica var. biflora*	*N. sylvatica*	5	OBL	D	Swamp tupelo
Paederia	*foetida*	*P. foetida*	2	na	AD	Skunkvine
Panicum	*hemitomon*	*P. hemitomon*	5	OBL	na	Maidencane
Panicum	*repens*	*P. repens*	4	FACW	na	Torpedograss
Panicum	*rigidulum*	*P. rigidulum*	4	FACW	OD	Redtop panicum
Parthenocissus	*quinquefolia*	*P. quinquefolia*	na	na	na	Virginia creeper
Paspalidium	*geminatum*	*P. geminatum*	5	OBL	na	Kissimmeegrass
Paspalum	*distichum*	*P. distichum*	5	OBL	na	Knotgrass
Persea	*palustris*	*P. palustris*	5	OBL	OD	Swamp bay
Pinus	*elliottii*	*P. elliottii*	2	UPL	AD	Slash pine
Pinus	*clausa*	*P. clausa*	1	UPL	U	Sand pine
Pluchea	*baccharis*	*P. baccharis*	4	FACW	OD	Rosy camphorweed
Polygonum	*hydropiperoides*	*P. hydropiperoides*	5	OBL	OD	Swamp smartweed
Pontederia	*cordata*	*P. cordata*	5	OBL	na	Pickerelweed
Proserpinaca	*pectinata*	*P. pectinata*	5	OBL	na	Combleaf mermaidweed
Quercus	*laurifolia*	*Q. laurifolia*	3	FACW	T	Laurel oak
Quercus	*nigra*	*Q. nigra*	3	FACW	T	Water oak
Quercus	*virginiana*	*Q. virginiana*	1	UPL	U	Live oak
Rhynchospora	*miliacea*	*R. miliacea*	5	OBL	na	Millet beaksedge
Rhynchospora	*cephalantha*	*R. cephalantha*	5	OBL	na	Bunched beaksedge
Rhynchospora	*inundata*	*R. inundata*	5	OBL	na	Narrowfruit horned beaksedge
Sabal	*palmetto*	*S. palmetto*	3	FAC	na	Cabbage palm
Saccharum	*giganteum*	*S. giganteum*	5	OBL	OD	Sugarcane plumegrass
Sacciolepis	*striata*	*S. striata*	4	FACW	na	American cupscale
Sagittaria	*lancifolia*	*S. lancifolia*	5	OBL	na	Bulltongue arrowhead
Saururus	*cernuus*	*S. cernuus*	5	OBL	na	Lizard's tail
Scleria	*sp.*	*Scleria sp.*	4	FACW	na	Nutrush
Scoparia	*dulcis*	*S. dulcis*	2	FAC	AD	Sweetbroom
Serenoa	*repens*	*S. repens*	1	UPL	na	Saw palmetto
Smilax	*bona-nox*	*S. bona-nox*	2	na	AD	Saw greenbrier
Smilax	*sp.*	*Smilax sp.*	2	UPL	AD	Greenbrier
Sphagnum	*sp.*	*Sphagnum sp.*	na	na	na	Moss
Stillingia	*aquatica*	*S. aquatica*	5	OBL	D	Water toothleaf
Syngonanthus	*flavidulus*	*S. flavidulus*	4	FACW	na	Yellow hatpins
Taxodium	*ascendens*	*T. ascendens*	5	OBL	D	Pond-cypress
Taxodium	*distichum*	*T. distichum*	5	OBL	D	Bald-cypress
Toxicodendron	*radicans*	*T. radicans*	2	na	AD	Eastern poison ivy
Ulmus	*americana*	*U. americana*	3	FACW	T	American elm
Utricularia	*sp.*	*Utricularia sp.*	5	OBL	na	Bladderworts
Vaccinium	*arboreum*	*V. arboreum*	na	na	na	Farkleberry
Vitis	*rotundifolia*	*V. rotundifolia*	2	na	AD	Muscadine
Woodwardia	*virginica*	*W. virginica*	4	FACW	na	Virginia chainfern
Xyris	*jupicai*	*X. jupicai*	4	FACW	na	Richard's yelloweyed grass

Appendix 2.   Estimated area and volume of water corresponding to stage and depth below land surface elevation at the wetland perimeter of Green Swamp Cypress.

[Stage, elevation in feet above North American Vertical Datum of 1988. Area and volume values derived using SURFER]

Depth	Stage	Area (acres)	Volume (acre-feet)	Percent of total wetland area flooded
0	97.7	1.670	0.81	100
0.1	97.6	1.490	0.65	89
0.2	97.5	1.190	0.52	71
0.3	97.4	0.940	0.41	56
0.4	97.3	0.760	0.33	46
0.5	97.2	0.640	0.26	38
0.6	97.1	0.550	0.20	33
0.7	97.0	0.450	0.15	27
0.8	96.9	0.370	0.10	22
0.9	96.8	0.300	0.071	18
1.0	96.7	0.230	0.045	14
1.1	96.6	0.160	0.025	10
1.2	96.5	0.085	0.013	5
1.3	96.4	0.050	0.007	3
1.4	96.3	0.029	0.003	2
1.5	96.2	0.012	0.001	1
1.6	96.1	0.002	0.000	<1
1.7	96.0	0.000	0.000	0

Appendix 3.   Estimated area and volume of water corresponding to stage and depth below land surface elevation at the wetland perimeter of New River Marsh.

[Stage, elevation in feet above North American Vertical Datum of 1988. Area and volume values derived using ArcMap tools]

Depth	Stage	Area (acres)	Volume (acre-feet)	Percent of total wetland area flooded
0	44.0	2.873	4.305	100
0.1	43.9	2.767	4.023	96
0.2	43.8	2.678	3.751	93
0.3	43.7	2.597	3.487	90
0.4	43.6	2.520	3.231	88
0.5	43.5	2.445	2.983	85
0.6	43.4	2.370	2.742	83
0.7	43.3	2.296	2.509	80
0.8	43.2	2.219	2.283	77
0.9	43.1	2.141	2.065	75
1.0	43.0	2.064	1.855	72
1.1	42.9	1.987	1.652	69
1.2	42.8	1.911	1.457	67
1.3	42.7	1.831	1.270	64
1.4	42.6	1.742	1.092	61
1.5	42.5	1.655	0.922	58
1.6	42.4	1.562	0.761	54
1.7	42.3	1.459	0.610	51
1.8	42.2	1.345	0.469	47
1.9	42.1	1.219	0.341	42
2.0	42.0	1.054	0.227	37
2.1	41.9	0.823	0.132	29
2.2	41.8	0.540	0.064	19
2.3	41.7	0.265	0.025	9
2.4	41.6	0.095	0.008	3
2.5	41.5	0.029	0.002	1
2.6	41.4	0.007	0.001	<1
2.7	41.3	0.003	0.000	<1
2.8	41.2	0.001	0.000	<1
2.9	41.1	0.000	0.000	0

Appendix 4.   Estimated area and volume of water corresponding to stage and depth below land surface elevation at the wetland perimeter of Q-1.

[Stage, elevation in feet above North American Vertical Datum of 1988. Area and volume values derived using ArcMap tools]

Depth	Stage	Area (acres)	Volume (acre-feet)	Percent of total wetland area flooded
0	73.4	1.444	1.039	100
0.1	73.3	1.319	0.901	91
0.2	73.2	1.213	0.775	84
0.3	73.1	1.113	0.659	77
0.4	73.0	1.016	0.552	70
0.5	72.9	0.921	0.455	64
0.6	72.8	0.827	0.368	57
0.7	72.7	0.735	0.290	51
0.8	72.6	0.638	0.221	44
0.9	72.5	0.539	0.162	37
1.0	72.4	0.437	0.114	30
1.1	72.3	0.346	0.074	24
1.2	72.2	0.257	0.044	18
1.3	72.1	0.172	0.023	12
1.4	72.0	0.102	0.009	7
1.5	71.9	0.042	0.002	3
1.6	71.8	0.004	0.000	0

Appendix 5.   Estimated area and volume of water corresponding to stage and depth below land surface elevation at the wetland perimeter of W-17.

[Stage, elevation in feet above North American Vertical Datum of 1988. Area and volume values derived using ArcMap tools]

Depth	Stage	Area (acres)	Volume (acre-feet)	Percent of total wetland area flooded
0	63.9	3.949	4.067	100
0.1	63.8	3.725	3.684	94
0.2	63.7	3.536	3.321	90
0.3	63.6	3.357	2.976	85
0.4	63.5	3.183	2.649	81
0.5	63.4	3.007	2.340	76
0.6	63.3	2.830	2.048	72
0.7	63.2	2.634	1.775	67
0.8	63.1	2.433	1.521	62
0.9	63.0	2.202	1.289	56
1.0	62.9	1.922	1.083	49
1.1	62.8	1.703	0.902	43
1.2	62.7	1.500	0.742	38
1.3	62.6	1.319	0.602	33
1.4	62.5	1.165	0.478	29
1.5	62.4	0.986	0.370	25
1.6	62.3	0.825	0.280	21
1.7	62.2	0.697	0.204	18
1.8	62.1	0.587	0.140	15
1.9	62.0	0.466	0.087	12
2.0	61.9	0.336	0.047	9
2.1	61.8	0.194	0.021	5
2.2	61.7	0.083	0.007	2
2.3	61.6	0.021	0.002	1
2.4	61.5	0.006	0.001	<1
2.5	61.4	0.000	0.000	0

Appendix 6.   Estimated area and volume of water corresponding to stage and depth below land surface elevation at the wetland perimeter of W-33.

[Stage, elevation in feet above North American Vertical Datum of 1988. Area and volume values derived from ArcMap tools]

Depth	Stage	Area (acres)	Volume (acre-feet)	Percent of total wetland area flooded
0	69.6	1.164	0.744	100
0.1	69.5	1.092	0.630	94
0.2	69.4	0.990	0.526	85
0.3	69.3	0.893	0.432	77
0.4	69.2	0.799	0.347	69
0.5	69.1	0.705	0.272	61
0.6	69.0	0.619	0.206	53
0.7	68.9	0.533	0.148	46
0.8	68.8	0.420	0.100	36
0.9	68.7	0.323	0.063	28
1.0	68.6	0.238	0.035	20
1.1	68.5	0.142	0.016	12
1.2	68.4	0.069	0.006	6
1.3	68.3	0.024	0.001	2
1.4	68.2	0.004	0.000	<1
1.5	68.1	0.000	0.000	0

Appendix 7.   Estimated area and volume of water corresponding to stage and depth below land surface elevation at the wetland perimeter of W-41.

[Stage, elevation in feet above North American Vertical Datum of 1988. Area and volume values derived using ArcMap tools]

Depth	Stage	Area (acres)	Volume (acre-feet)	Percent of total wetland area flooded
0	75.2	4.280	4.740	100
0.1	75.1	4.043	4.337	94
0.2	75.0	3.805	3.933	89
0.3	74.9	3.597	3.573	84
0.4	74.8	3.388	3.213	79
0.5	74.7	3.188	2.895	74
0.6	74.6	2.988	2.576	70
0.7	74.5	2.813	2.295	66
0.8	74.4	2.637	2.014	62
0.9	74.3	2.466	1.768	58
1.0	74.2	2.294	1.521	54
1.1	74.1	2.106	1.310	49
1.2	74.0	1.917	1.098	45
1.3	73.9	1.717	0.927	40
1.4	73.8	1.517	0.755	35
1.5	73.7	1.310	0.625	31
1.6	73.6	1.102	0.494	26
1.7	73.5	0.957	0.399	22
1.8	73.4	0.811	0.304	19
1.9	73.3	0.684	0.236	16
2.0	73.2	0.557	0.168	13
2.1	73.1	0.447	0.124	10
2.2	73.0	0.337	0.080	8
2.3	72.9	0.257	0.054	6
2.4	72.8	0.176	0.028	4
2.5	72.7	0.117	0.017	3
2.6	72.6	0.057	0.006	1
2.7	72.5	0.000	0.000	0

Appendix 8. Estimated area and volume of water corresponding to stage and depth below land surface elevation at the wetland perimeter of W-56.

[Stage, elevation in feet above North American Vertical Datum of 1988. Area and volume values derived from ArcMap tools]

Depth	Stage	Area (acres)	Volume (acre-feet)	Percent of total wetland area flooded
0	63.7	0.716	0.538	100
0.1	63.6	0.685	0.468	96
0.2	63.5	0.654	0.401	91
0.3	63.4	0.622	0.337	87
0.4	63.3	0.585	0.277	82
0.5	63.2	0.540	0.221	75
0.6	63.1	0.484	0.169	68
0.7	63.0	0.416	0.124	58
0.8	62.9	0.343	0.086	48
0.9	62.8	0.267	0.056	37
1.0	62.7	0.199	0.032	28
1.1	62.6	0.128	0.016	18
1.2	62.5	0.058	0.007	8
1.3	62.4	0.025	0.003	4
1.4	62.3	0.012	0.001	2
1.5	62.2	0.005	0.000	1
1.6	62.1	0.002	0.000	0

Appendix 9. Estimated area and volume of water corresponding to stage and depth below land surface elevation at the wetland perimeter of Starkey D.

[Stage, elevation in feet above North American Vertical Datum of 1988. Area and volumes derived Using ArcMap tools]

Depth	Stage	Area (acres)	Volume (acre-feet)	Percent of total wetland area flooded
0	31.1	5.327	7.135	100
0.2	30.9	4.924	6.097	92
0.4	30.7	4.406	5.165	83
0.6	30.5	3.842	4.339	72
0.8	30.3	3.307	3.623	62
1.0	30.1	2.765	3.018	52
1.2	29.9	2.356	2.508	44
1.4	29.7	2.026	2.071	38
1.6	29.5	1.715	1.697	32
1.8	29.3	1.443	1.382	27
2.0	29.1	1.145	1.124	21
2.2	28.9	0.903	0.920	17
2.4	28.7	0.731	0.757	14
2.6	28.5	0.646	0.620	12
2.8	28.3	0.570	0.499	11
3.0	28.1	0.495	0.392	9
3.2	27.9	0.428	0.300	8
3.4	27.7	0.371	0.220	7
3.6	27.5	0.312	0.152	6
3.8	27.3	0.250	0.095	5
4.0	27.1	0.186	0.052	3
4.2	26.9	0.121	0.021	2
4.4	26.7	0.044	0.004	1
4.6	26.5	0.006	0.000	<1
4.7	26.4	0.000	0.000	0

Appendix 10.   Estimated area and volume of water corresponding to stage and depth below land surface elevation at the wetland perimeter of Starkey E.

[Stage, elevation in feet above North American Vertical Datum of 1988. Area and volume values derived using ArcMap tools]

Depth	Stage	Area (acres)	Volume (acre-feet)	Percent of total wetland area flooded
0	38.0	3.416	15.394	100
0.5	37.5	3.414	13.394	99
1.0	37.0	3.052	12.040	89
1.5	36.5	2.739	10.598	80
2.0	36.0	2.512	9.287	74
2.5	35.5	2.302	8.084	67
3.0	35.0	2.106	6.983	62
3.5	34.5	1.924	5.976	56
4.0	34.0	1.755	5.057	51
4.5	33.5	1.601	4.218	47
5.0	33.0	1.451	3.454	42
5.5	32.5	1.290	2.769	38
6.0	32.0	1.123	2.166	33
6.5	31.5	0.957	1.646	28
7.0	31.0	0.796	1.208	23
7.5	30.5	0.649	0.848	19
8.0	30.0	0.518	0.556	15
8.5	29.5	0.398	0.328	12
9.0	29.0	0.265	0.161	8
9.5	28.5	0.116	0.069	3
10.0	28.0	0.044	0.031	1
10.5	27.5	0.027	0.013	<1
11.0	27.0	0.013	0.003	<1
11.5	26.5	0.002	0.000	0
11.9	26.1	0.000	0.000	0

Appendix 11.   Estimated area and volume of water corresponding to stage and depth below land surface elevation at the wetland perimeter of Starkey N.

[Stage, elevation in feet above North American Vertical Datum of 1988. Area and volume values derived using ArcMap tools.]

Depth	Stage	Area (acres)	Volume (acre-feet)	Percent of total wetland area flooded
0	46.5	3.923	2.632	100
0.1	46.4	3.741	2.248	95
0.2	46.3	3.559	1.883	91
0.3	46.2	3.378	1.537	86
0.4	46.1	3.170	1.209	81
0.5	46.0	2.930	0.904	75
0.6	45.9	2.617	0.625	67
0.7	45.8	2.103	0.389	54
0.8	45.7	1.424	0.211	36
0.9	45.6	0.639	0.113	16
1.0	45.5	0.340	0.066	9
1.1	45.4	0.201	0.040	5
1.2	45.3	0.136	0.023	3
1.3	45.2	0.086	0.012	2
1.4	45.1	0.049	0.005	1
1.5	45.0	0.024	0.002	1
1.6	44.9	0.008	0.000	0

Appendix 12.   Estimated area and volume of water corresponding to stage and depth below land surface elevation at the wetland perimeter of Starkey 108.

[Stage, elevation in feet above North American Vertical Datum of 1988. Area and volume values derived using ArcMap tools]

Depth	Stage	Area (acres)	Volume (acre-feet)	Percent of total wetland area flooded
0	44.8	1.081	0.671	100
0.1	44.7	0.984	0.567	91
0.2	44.6	0.899	0.474	83
0.3	44.5	0.821	0.388	76
0.4	44.4	0.747	0.309	69
0.5	44.3	0.658	0.239	61
0.6	44.2	0.565	0.177	52
0.7	44.1	0.447	0.127	41
0.8	44.0	0.341	0.087	32
0.9	43.9	0.254	0.058	24
1.0	43.8	0.178	0.036	16
1.1	43.7	0.117	0.022	11
1.2	43.6	0.076	0.012	7
1.3	43.5	0.049	0.006	4
1.4	43.4	0.026	0.002	2
1.5	43.3	0.009	0.001	1
1.6	43.2	0.002	0.000	0
1.7	43.1	0.000	0.000	0